Promoting Language Through Physical Education

Using Sign Language and Spanish to Engage Everyone

Luis Columna, PhD

Syracuse University

Lauren Lieberman, PhD

The College at Brockport

Human Kinetics

Library of Congress Cataloging-in-Publication Data

Columna, Luis.
  Promoting language through physical education : using sign language and Spanish to engage everyone / Luis Columna, Lauren Lieberman.
      p. cm.
  Includes bibliographical references.
  ISBN-13: 978-0-7360-9451-1 (soft cover)
  ISBN-10: 0-7360-9451-2 (soft cover)
  1. Physical education and training--Study and teaching--United States. 2. Physical education and training--Curricula--United States. 3. Sign language--Study and teaching--United States. 4. Sign language acquisition--United States. 5. Spanish language--Study and teaching--United States. 6. Language and languages--Study and teaching--United States. 7. Second language acquisition--United States. I. Title.
  GV365.C645 2011
  613.707--dc22

                                                    2011014348

ISBN-10: 0-7360-9451-2
ISBN-13: 978-0-7360-9451-1

Acquisitions Editor: Scott Wikgren; **Managing Editor:** Amy Stahl; **Assistant Editor:** Rachel Brito; **Copyeditor:** Jan Feeney; **Graphic Designer:** Nancy Rasmus; **Graphic Artist:** Yvonne Griffith; **Cover Designer:** Keith Blomberg; **DVD Face Designer:** Susan Rothermel Allen; **Photographer (cover):** Jason Allen and Human Kinetics; **Photographer (back cover):** William Turk; **Photographer (interior):** Luis Columna, unless otherwise noted; **Photo Asset Manager:** Laura Fitch; **Photo Production Manager:** Jason Allen; **Art Manager:** Kelly Hendren; **Associate Art Manager:** Alan L. Wilborn; **Illustrations:** © Human Kinetics; **Printer:** United Graphics

The contents of this DVD are licensed for educational public performance for viewing by a traditional (live) audience, via closed circuit television, or via computerized local area networks within a single building or geographically unified campus. To request a license to broadcast these contents to a wider audience—for example, throughout a school district or state, or on a television station—please contact your sales representative (**www.HumanKinetics.com/SalesRepresentatives**).

Printed in the United States of America   10 9 8 7 6 5 4 3 2 1

The paper in this book is certified under a sustainable forestry program.

Human Kinetics
Web site: www.HumanKinetics.com

United States: Human Kinetics
P.O. Box 5076
Champaign, IL 61825-5076
800-747-4457
e-mail: humank@hkusa.com

Canada: Human Kinetics
475 Devonshire Road Unit 100
Windsor, ON N8Y 2L5
800-465-7301 (in Canada only)
e-mail: info@hkcanada.com

Europe: Human Kinetics
107 Bradford Road, Stanningley
Leeds LS28 6AT, United Kingdom
+44 (0) 113 255 5665
e-mail: hk@hkeurope.com

Australia: Human Kinetics
57A Price Avenue
Lower Mitcham, South Australia 5062
08 8372 0999
e-mail: info@hkaustralia.com

New Zealand: Human Kinetics
P.O. Box 80, Torrens Park, South Australia 5062
0800 222 062
e-mail: info@hknewzealand.com

E5153

To all the school-age children in North America who are not native English speakers and who value social interaction and friendship.

contents

contributors vii • foreword ix • acknowledgments xi • how to use the
DVD xiii • DVD contents xv

introduction   1

part I   Importance of Learning About Diversity

one   **Learning About Deaf Culture**   7
uno

two   **Learning About Hispanic Culture**   15
dos

part II   Importance of Infusing Language Into Physical Activity Programs

three   **Infusing Language Into Physical Education**   23
tres

four   **Assessing Learning**   29
cuatro

five   **Elementary School Activities**   35
cinco

six   **Middle School Activities**   45
seis

seven   **High School Activities**   53
siete

part III   Spanish and Sign Language Dictionaries

eight   **Spanish Words for Physical Education**   63
ocho

nine   **ASL Signs for Physical Education**   75
nueve

appendix A 81 • appendix B 83 • references 85 •
about the authors 87 • DVD-ROM user instructions 88

contributors

Rebecca K. Lytle, PhD, is a professor and chair of the department of kinesiology at California State University (CSU) at Chico. She has presented at numerous state, national, and international conferences and has received many awards, including the 2008 Professional Achievement Honor from CSU for excellence in teaching and significant contributions to the discipline. She also chaired the Adapted Physical Activity Council of the American Association for Physical Activity and Recreation. In 2005 she received the Recognition Award for Autism Sensory and Motor Clinic from the Autism Society of Northern California.

Margarita Fernández-Vivó, PhD, is an associate professor in the department of physical education at the University of Puerto Rico at Mayagüez. She obtained her PhD in physical education teacher education from Florida State University. Her interests are physical education teacher education and adapted physical education. Since 2007 Dr. Fernández-Vivó has directed CAAMP Abilities in Puerto Rico.

Patricia Martínez de la Vega Mansilla is a full-time lecturer IV at the State University of New York College at Cortland, where she has been teaching Spanish and ESL. Her specializations are educational psychology, Spanish, ESL, and the teaching of methodology courses for teaching foreign languages in elementary school. Her research with Dr. Paulo Quaglio focuses on the pragmatic use of corpus linguistics in the language classroom. Before teaching at SUNY Cortland, Ms. Martínez de la Vega Mansilla taught English as a foreign language in Mexico City, where she was also the academic coordinator of a language institute and a teacher at an immersion program at the elementary school level.

Kathleen "Kat" Ellis, PhD, is an associate professor of kinesiology at West Chester University in Pennsylvania. Her specializations are adapted physical education and disability studies, with main research foci on deafness and Deaf sport. Before coming to WCUPA, Dr. Ellis was the adapted physical education coordinator at the University of Rhode Island for seven years. She holds dual PhDs in both kinesiology (specializing in adapted physical education) and Deaf education from Michigan State University.

Carah Taylor is a physical education teacher at Rochester School for the Deaf in New York. She has published articles in the Journal of Physical Education, Recreation and Dance. Carah holds an MSED in adapted physical education from State University of New York College at Brockport. She lives in Rochester with her husband and two kids.

Student Contributors

Nicole Corcoran

Joanna Depace

Kathleen Reid

Aaron Hutchins

Lauren Friedlander

Jeff Yellen

Tiffany Mitrakos

Francesca Futia

Wellington De Jesus

Rhonda Morse

foreword

The National Commission on Teaching and America's Future (1996) stressed the importance of *all* children and youths learning from competent and caring teachers. One of the biggest challenges for such teachers is associated with North America's increasingly diverse society. Teachers must be able to teach and work with the various cultures that students in their schools represent. Teachers are responsible for educating all students, regardless of ethnicity, race, socioeconomic status, gender, language, disability, religion, sexual orientation, and geographical origination. Teachers who take into account this array of diversity in their teaching are culturally responsive educators.

Becoming a culturally responsive teacher is no simple task. The richness that cultural diversity brings to an educational setting adds to the complexity of teaching. Consider some of the available data: More than 90 percent of classroom teachers in the United States are white, middle class, and monolingual English speakers (Lee & Kumashiro, 2005). Yet, students of color will make up about 50 percent of the U.S. school population by 2020 (Culp, Chepyator-Thomson, & Hsu, 2009). More than 45 million school-aged children (more than 1 in 5) live in non-English-dominant households (NAEYC, 1995). Nearly 13 percent of school-aged children are classified as disabled and are mainstreamed (i.e., placed in inclusive settings) (Aud et al., 2010; U.S. Department of Education, 2002).

The focus of this book is unique because it deals with issues of diversity specific to language and communication modes in physical education and physical activity settings. Most of us see the word *communication* and automatically think of the English language being spoken and heard. However, as culturally responsive teachers, we must acknowledge that some of our students are non-English speakers and some students are hard of hearing or deaf. How is it that we can actually teach children who don't speak "our" language or can't audibly hear what we are saying? How can we learn about our students and establish a mutual respect if we don't know how to communicate in those students' languages?

Effective teachers are able to maintain open lines of communication with their students. Students are more likely to listen and hear if they believe that their teachers are sincerely interested in them as learners and as individuals. One way that you can do this is by learning how to communicate using an alternative language, such as Spanish or American Sign Language. If you are truly trying to learn about certain students out of sincere caring and a desire to facilitate those students' educational experiences, they will become more engaged in learning and will be more inclined to participate in setting goals. Consequently, they will believe in the opportunities for continued learning. Positive experiences and effective communication are especially important in physical education and physical activity settings where learning can be planned for and perceived as fun and can form the basis for lifelong habits of health and wellness.

Authors Luis Columna and Lauren Lieberman provide strategies to help you infuse alternative forms of language into your programs. *Promoting Language Through Physical Education* is a valuable resource for teachers at all grade levels and for preservice teachers who strive to become effective, culturally responsive practitioners. It will be very useful for facilitating students' learning, especially for students whose mode of communication differs from your own. Learning to communicate in alternative forms of language takes you one step closer to truly being a competent, caring teacher and ensures that *all* students have an equal opportunity to learn what you are teaching. Columna and Lieberman are to be commended for their effort in helping teachers in physical education and physical activity settings achieve this goal.

Luz M. Cruz, EdD

acknowledgments

The authors would like to thank the contributors of this book and Dr. Alisa James, Dr. Luz Cruz, and Monica Kleeman for reviewing the book. Lauren would like to thank her partner Katrina Arndt for her continued support and encouragement. Luis would like to thank his family, colleagues and former students at the State University of New York at Cortland, and his advisors Dr. Jean Pyfer and Dr. Carol Huettig for being supportive during his graduate experience.

how to use the DVD

The DVD included in this book encompasses five parts. You will find the physical education signs, the Spanish words tables, sign language word tables, as well as the appendixes of the book. As you read this book be sure to note where the DVD icon **DVD** is as that is when you should refer to the DVD for additional information in these areas.

When you are teaching be sure to review either the signs or the Spanish words located in the tables or in the DVD before you teach. This way you can be comfortable knowing how to read, pronouncing and/or signing the words. To view the proper spelling of the words being signed or the Spanish words being pronounced on the DVD, turn on the subtitle feature on your DVD player. For the Spanish translations, the verbs are shown in the infinitive, but they are also conjugated into the singular and plural command forms. The (s.) next to the conjugated verb symbolizes the singular form while (pl.) means plural. Please note that an additional treat for teachers is the website www.ASLPro.com. This website can be used as a supplement to the DVD and tables in this book. In addition, ASL Pro can be downloaded into your phone or iPad for a minimal fee. The benefit of having this application on your iPad or your phone is that you can bring technology into your classroom to enhance your signing abilities. For Spanish you can also use supplemental resources to this book such as Google Translate.

DVD contents

Sign Language Video Clips

Nouns
- Bathroom
- Water
- Friend
- Rest
- Help

Adjectives
- Tired
- Slow
- Fast
- Difficult
- Soft
- Hard

Phrases
- No.
- Yes.
- I'm sorry.
- Please.
- Thank you.

Praise
- Good job.
- Awesome.
- Wrong
- Skilled
- More effort

Verbs
- Finished
- Line up
- Pay attention or look at me
- Stop
- Come here
- Bend your body
- Bend your knees
- Sit
- Stand
- Hurt
- Jump
- Hop
- Run
- Walk
- Gallop
- Skip
- Kick
- Pass
- Catch
- Throw
- Swim

Directions
- Overhand
- Underhand
- Out
- In
- Over
- Under
- Through

Colors
- Colors
- Green
- Blue
- Yellow
- Red
- Orange
- Purple
- Pink
- Black
- Brown

Feelings
- Feelings
- Happy
- Sad
- Mad or angry
- Don't like
- Like

Sports
- Lacrosse
- Basketball
- Baseball
- Softball
- Volleyball
- Soccer
- Hockey
- Football
- Wrestling
- Tennis
- Bat
- Ball

Spanish Video Clips

Nouns
- Bathroom
- Water
- Friend
- Rest
- Help

Adjectives
- Tired
- Slow
- Fast
- Difficult
- Soft
- Hard

Phrases
No.
Yes.
I'm sorry.
Please.
Thank you.
Praise
Good job.
Awesome.
Wrong
Skilled
More effort
Verbs
Finished
Line up
Pay attention
Stop
Come here
Bend your body
Bend your knees
Sit
Stand
Hurt
Jump
Hop
Run
Walk
Gallop
Skip
Kick
Pass
Catch
Throw
Swim
Directions
Overhand
Underhand
Out
In
Over
Under
Through
Colors
Colors
Green
Blue
Yellow
Red
Orange
Purple
Pink
Black
Brown
Feelings
Feelings
Happy
Sad

Mad or angry
Don't like
Like
Sports
Lacrosse
Basketball
Baseball
Softball
Volleyball
Soccer
Hockey
Football
Wrestling
Tennis
Bat
Ball

Sign Language Physical Education Dictionaries
Words and Phrases
Execution Feedback
Directions
Physical Education Vocabulary
Movement Feedback
Game Terminology
Physical Education Formations and Commands
Feelings
Items and Gender
Colors

Spanish Words Physical Education Dictionaries
Vowel Phonemes
Sample Pronunciations of Vowel Phonemes
Body Parts
Clothing and Gender and Possession
Colors and Directions
Telling Time
Equipment
Family
Days of the Week
Months of the Year
Greetings
Numbers
Praise
Questions
Seasons and Weather
Verbs

Reproducibles
Figure 4.1: Self-Assessment Examples
Figure 4.2: Peer-Assessment Checklist
Appendix A: Resources
Appendix B: Softball Homework Sheet
How to Use the DVD

Credits

Introduction

North America's ethnic diversity is on the rise, along with the number of people who speak languages other than English. Therefore, especially in our schools, it is important to create an atmosphere that welcomes everyone.

The main function of any language is communication. Communication is an exchange of thoughts, ideas, and feelings. It is a process involving interactions in which individuals negotiate meanings to acquire and exchange information. Every language is composed of conventionalized signs, symbols, semiotic rules, gestures, and sounds that are put together in a certain order to transmit ideas. Knowing the words to use in each situation, what is appropriate and inappropriate, and how to pronounce words is of the utmost importance in understanding and being understood by others.

All languages have productive and receptive components. *Productive* language is the ability to produce language in any of a number of modalities such as speech, hand signs, or writing. *Receptive* language is the ability to understand spoken, written, or visual communication. In order for children to become comfortable using any language, they must learn both receptive and productive skills. In many cases, productive language is more difficult to learn and to use. It is also more difficult to assess because it requires more individual (one-on-one) instruction from educators to ensure that students can use language appropriately.

Students whose primary means of communication is not English participate in recreation, sport, and physical education programs. Professionals providing services to those students often encounter problems because, in many cases, professionals are not able to communicate with their participants and vice versa.

Promoting Language Through Physical Education provides teachers, professionals, parents, administrators, and professors with strategies for integrating non-English speakers into educational settings. Settings for learning include physical education, physical activity, aquatics, recreation, fitness, outdoor education, and camp programs. In this book, we use sign language and Spanish language as two examples of how you can integrate other languages into a curriculum. However, the ideas in this book can be used with other languages as well.

This book presents the use of language for enhancing lessons and developing culturally responsive pedagogy. In incorporating this approach, you must use careful planning and take time learning words and phrases for each lesson. Because you are infusing language into your lessons, you want students to understand the content and learn correct pronunciation. **DVD** This book also provides the readers with a bound-in DVD that provides videos of American sign language signs and correct pronunciation of Spanish terms commonly used in physical education.

Physical education is a subject area that is well suited for integrating language concepts. In a typical physical education class, you might encounter diverse groups of students who communicate in various ways, including speaking Spanish and using sign language. We propose the use of words and formulaic expressions in Spanish or sign language vocabulary to communicate with those students. Formulaic expressions are already-existing phrases, single words, or several words acting as a unit, which may not be changed (e.g., *in other words*, *thanks a lot*, and *as far as I know*).

The main objective of this book is *not* to teach you or your students a language but to help you use other languages to *enhance* communication among students and between students and teachers. Non-English-speaking, Deaf, and hard-of-hearing students typically go through a transition period in mainstream education (i.e., learning a second language and learning to read lips). Using some sign language and Spanish (or any other language) in physical education classes as part of the content-based learning provides multiple benefits for the entire learning community: It enhances the foreign language skills of the non-Spanish-speaking population, promotes open-mindedness, and enhances students' understanding of other cultures. This understanding will in turn create a stronger community and a better society for all students. Another benefit of infusing language into the curriculum is that it allows your school to comply with the educational standards of various disciplines at one time in a contextualized way that communicates some interesting information to the students. The infusion of language into physical education facilitates learning of cross-curricular content while reinforcing basic movement and fitness concepts.

Infusing language learning in your teaching sends a strong welcoming message to those native speakers and helps create a community in which all children feel valued. Any amount of language education is richer when taught with cultural content. You will be able to make your lessons more innovative through language infusion. Integration of various modes of communication allows students the opportunity to communicate with other students who speak different languages. This might trigger their curiosity to learn more about another language and culture. But keep in mind that, in order to infuse language into your class, you do not have to have a student in your class who speaks Spanish or uses sign language.

In addition this practice also demonstrates appropriate culturally responsive teaching practices. Culturally responsive pedagogy is the ability to accept others' beliefs and values and integrate appropriate practices into educational settings (Cagle, 2006). Individuals who implement this pedagogy use the "cultural knowledge, prior experiences, frames of references, and performance styles" of culturally, ethnically, linguistically, and economically diverse students "to make learning encounters more relevant to and effective for them" (Gay, 2000, p. 29).

Physical education is often the favorite subject area among students. In physical activity environments, children interact with each other and express emotions. Play enriches children's language development and helps them extend their language use, especially while interacting with peers in play dialogues (Wilford, 2003). In order for learning to take place, the material presented must be meaningful to the students. For example, if you are emphasizing colors in Spanish, you could instruct children to move on scooters to the red (rojo) hula hoops, then the green (verde), then the yellow (amarillo). This way, very little time is spent focusing on the words, but the concepts of the colors are embedded into the lesson.

This book is organized into three parts. Part I highlights the importance of language and the value of culture. Chapter 1 discusses various aspects of Deaf culture. Chapter 2 explores Hispanic culture and its prominence in North America. Chapter 3 discusses strategies you can use in infusing language into your physical activity lessons. Part II explores infusing language into physical activity settings. Chapter 4 contains information on assessment of learning. Developmentally appropriate activities for elementary, middle school, and high school students are presented in chapters 5, 6, and 7, respectively. Descriptions of the activities, equipment needed, and practice words are presented in these chapters. Part III (chapters 8 and 9) contains the Spanish and sign language dictionaries to support you in your instruction of programs or classes. The vocabulary presented in these chapters is organized by movement concepts and games and activities. For the Spanish translations, the verbs are shown in the infinitive, but they are also conjugated into the singular and plural command forms. The (s.) next to the conjugated verb symbolizes the singular form while (pl.) means plural. Included in this book is a list of references and two appendixes. **DVD** Appendix A contains a list of websites that you can refer to in your work. The sites include videos of professionals executing signs, pronunciations, and translations. Appendix B presents an example of an assignment that can be sent home.

Infusing languages into physical activity programs is not difficult with the Internet at your fingertips, and it is a wonderful way for students and faculty to collaborate. The intersections among language, literacy, and physical activity, especially in terms of supporting the learning of children whose primary language is not English, need to be seen as a goal of creating inclusive settings.

Importance of Learning About Diversity

Part I presents a rationale for learning about diversity and being able to communicate with learners of diverse backgrounds. In the United States, the number of people who use languages other than English, or in addition to English, is growing every day. Even though you might not have students of various cultural backgrounds in your classes, you will find it valuable to share with your students aspects of other cultures as well as languages. Part I of this book ensures that you have relevant information to share about Deaf and Hispanic cultures. Be sure to refer to the resources included at the end of this book for further information.

Chapter 1 presents information about the Deaf culture. Hearing loss is the number one disability in the United States. Therefore, at some time in your career as a physical educator, you will very likely instruct students who are hard of hearing or Deaf. This chapter also contains advice on etiquette when you're communicating with people in this cultural group.

Chapter 2 discusses the importance of learning about the Hispanic culture. The chapter also contains a brief history of Hispanic culture in the United States, including its role in sport and physical activity and physical educators' role in accommodating learners of this background.

one
uno

Learning About Deaf Culture

Hearing loss describes individuals who are hard of hearing or Deaf. Hearing loss is the number one disability in the United States. In many estimates, 1 in every 10 Americans, and 3 school-age children per 1,000, will have a hearing loss (HLA, 2007). Therefore, at some point in their careers, physical educators are very likely to instruct students who are hard of hearing or Deaf.

History of Deaf Culture

Culture is a pattern of beliefs, values, behaviors, arts, customs, institutions, social forms, and knowledge that are characteristic of a community (Schirmer, 2001). This definition, along with the history of other cultures, entails cultural influences of various aspects of American society (Moores, 2001). Deaf culture is no exception. Historically, residential schools for the deaf served as both the foundation and building blocks for Deaf community leading to the formation of a unique language as well as socialization, values, beliefs, and institutions. A result is an identification as a culture.

Deaf culture plays a critical role in the identification of Deaf children and adults as a minority group. To fully understand the Deaf culture, one must first distinguish between the use of Deaf (with an uppercase *d*) and deaf (with a lowercase *d*). Deaf (uppercase) is a term used solely to identify a cultural and linguistic minority. The word *deaf* with a lowercase *d* refers to the medical view of deafness as a disability, impairment of hearing, and a sole focus on the loss of hearing itself. In the medical view, deafness is seen from a perspective of disability, not a cultural perspective. Even though the medical aspect is a consideration, the social aspect of Deaf culture is one of the most important in physical education.

Deaf Sport and Its Relationship to Deaf Culture

One of the best ways to truly understand Deaf culture is to understand Deaf sport. Deaf sport encompasses all aspects of cultural characteristics and serves as a stepping-stone for many deaf individuals' becoming more aware of their identification as deaf people and the strong cohesion in the Deaf community.

> When making the connection between Deaf culture and sport, a quote from one of the most renowned experts in Deaf sport details its importance. Deaf sport can be thought of as a vehicle for understanding the dynamics of being Deaf. It facilitates a social identification among Deaf people that is not easily obtained in other sociocultural contexts. It relies on a Deaf perspective to define its social patterns of behaviors, and it presents an orientation to deafness that is different from that endorsed by hearing institutions. Essentially, Deaf sport emphasizes the honor of being Deaf, whereas society tends to focus on the adversity of deafness (Stewart, 1991).

When many people hear the term *Deaf sport* they think of small, unorganized activities in which people with hearing loss participate. As my partner told me when she first heard the phrase, "I was under the assumption that Deaf sport was just a bunch of deaf people getting together at the local ball field or park to partake in a recreational game or activity" (P. Andrews, personal communication, March 15, 2005). Many hearing people are not aware of the impact that Deaf sport has on not only the Deaf community but also hearing individuals who are somehow connected to Deaf individuals involved in sport. Many people, especially those who are hearing, lack experience and knowledge regarding Deaf sport and its influence and significance from a cultural and personal standpoint. Much of the research on Deaf sport has been directed toward an understanding of and appreciation for a cultural phenomenon so different from yet so similar to their own.

To gain an understanding of the importance of Deaf sport, one must use a global perspective rather than a single point of view. In this respect, an individual's understanding and experience in Deaf sport may be different depending on the level of involvement and awareness of its existence. In fact, to understand Deaf sport, one must consider it from several perspectives:

- A universal perspective
- A psychological and educational perspective
- As a social paradigm
- Lifelong participation in several roles
- Bridging of the gap between the deaf and hearing worlds
- Two critical aspects of Deaf sport: communication and socialization

Deaf sport is not just about sport (competing, winning or losing, or putting heart and soul into reaching the pinnacle of athletic abilities). It's so much more than that. It's about culture. It's about communicating using sign language. It's about a level of socialization a deaf person does not encounter in the hearing world. It's about a deaf person being on equal terms with all other people participating in, attending as spectators, and organizing the entire event. It's much, much bigger than many non-deaf people would expect. It's a sense of acceptance and accomplishment based solely on the athletic skills of the Deaf individuals involved.

Deaf sport is self-governed (i.e., it is run by only deaf athletes). There is a sense of achievement from the ground up, not only in that all athletes must have at least a 55-decibel hearing loss in their better ear and no hearing aids are allowed during competitions leading to the games, but also that the majority, if not all, of the people involved in the planning, organization, and administration of the games are Deaf themselves.

Universal Perspective of Deaf Sport

Deaf sport is the largest, most multifaceted event in the world controlled explicitly by Deaf individuals (Stewart, 1991). The scope of involvement and intensity differ across the spectrum based on the level of participation. At one end of the spectrum, Deaf sport can range from those backyard get-togethers of Deaf individuals enjoying each other's company while participating in a sport. On the other end of the spectrum is a professionally produced sporting event. As involvement across the spectrum increases, so does the intensity of participation. At the highest level, Deaf sport migrates into the international radar, bringing together deaf individuals from numerous countries vying for the top honors in their sport through participation in the Deaflympics, an international event rivaling the Olympics. The *only* difference between the Olympics and Deaflympics is that one is governed by hearing people and the other by Deaf people; however, one thing can be said about the autonomy of Deaf sport: A Deaf person can conceivably be involved in the Olympics at a high executive administrative level, but a hearing person cannot be involved in the governing of the Deaflympics (Deaflympics, 2005).

Deaf sport is a lifestyle for some people. Early involvement has opened doors to more in-depth participation as well as lifelong friendships. The universal perspective associated with Deaf sport involves valuable encounters with people from other countries and experiences with customs of various nations. This large congregation of Deaf people in a selected location for a common purpose is unique. In addition to the variety of people and nations involved over the years, a unique aspect is the ultimate experience of learning and being influenced by a diversity of sign languages. While sign language is not universal, Deaf sport is. From the local through the international levels, people who participate in and enjoy Deaf sport do so for similar reasons: competition, socialization, and communication.

Psychological Perspective of Deaf Sport

As a cultural and linguistic minority, many Deaf people have feelings of isolation in a predominantly hearing world. Even with the best accommodations, Deaf people tend not to feel the same sense of belonging as hearing people feel when involved in sports. In fact, during a time of critical psychological development,

Deaf Role Models

As mentioned earlier, the Deaflympics are similar to the Olympics. The only difference is that athletes have to be Deaf in order to compete in the Deaflympics. To be eligible to compete, players must have hearing loss of 55 decibels or more in their better ear without the use of hearing aids. In September 2009, the Deaflympics were held in Taipei, China. Two soccer players from both the U.S. women's and men's teams, Katie Romano and Mike Lawson, are wonderful role models (see figure 1.1).

Katie graduated from a mainstream school in Arizona. She played soccer for Gallaudet University. She also competed in the 2005 Deaflympics in Melbourne, Australia. Mike graduated from a mainstream school in New Jersey. He played soccer for the Rochester Institute of Technology. Mike also competed in the 2005 Deaflympics in Australia.

Figure 1.1   Mike Lawson is a player for the U.S. soccer team in the Deaflympics.

Photo courtesy of Michelle D. Dawson.

Katie and Mike are great athletes who are successful in life. Mike is teaching at a school for the deaf. Katie is also a teacher. Deaf people can be great at anything, and nothing can stop them from pursuing their dreams.

Deaf children in integrated educational settings may have lower levels of self-esteem and lack of social acceptance by their hearing peers than Deaf children attending schools for Deaf children (Mertens, 1989; Owers, 1996; Tvingstedt, 1995). "Essentially, among the most important motivations to participate in Deaf sport are the sense of belonging, the convenience of communicating in signs, the lack of similar opportunities in hearing sport, and the need to see oneself as being a worthy contributor to a community" (Stewart, 1991, p. 85).

Deaf individuals in the hearing world face daily frustrations in communication and interaction. Deaf sport allows for a release of those frustrations among members who share an appreciation for fellow participants. The understanding of the exclusiveness of being a Deaf person in a predominantly hearing world is crucial in Deaf sport.

Deaf sport in and of itself is an extension of Deaf culture. For example, Deaf sport allows for face-to-face interaction, which is a cornerstone of Deaf culture. In addition, Deaf sport affords opportunities for leadership roles. Deaf sport offers a sense of self within a compatible community, which makes signed communication natural.

Deaf sport is a way of asserting the strength of being deaf, displaying self-determination, and withstanding opposition from a hearing society to create a physical and social context for self-actualization. Through Deaf sport, the strength of the Deaf culture is displayed.

Educational Perspective of Deaf Sport

Just as the goal of physical education in schools is to promote lifelong physical activity and wellness, Deaf sport, even at the recreational level, allows for the opportunity to begin healthy habits that last a lifetime. This is a critical aspect of Deaf sport given that several studies have shown that Deaf children's fitness levels are lower than the fitness levels of their hearing peers (Goodman & Hopper, 1992; Pender & Patterson, 1982; Winnick & Short, 1985). The number of discrepancies in fitness that are due to communication issues is unknown, and studies taking communication modalities into account have reported contrasting results (Stewart, Dummer, & Haubenstricker, 1990). Socialization and communication are the two major cultural differences between Deaf and "hearing" sport, so perhaps the overall impact of Deaf sport on fitness has been underestimated.

Ellis (2001) completed a study that indicated that deaf children could be evaluated with the use of the same fitness standards as for their hearing peers. The major adaptation was to ensure the Deaf child's chosen communication modality was being implemented. The results of this study point to the fact that the standards set for hearing children work also for Deaf children. In fact, Stewart and Ellis (2006) reported that many of the same techniques and strategies for introducing healthy lifestyle habits to Deaf children are similar to those used with hearing children; the only major difference is in how the information was presented.

Many Deaf children are introduced to Deaf sport through Deaf role models. These people of influence may themselves be athletes or coaches or, better yet, parents who are aware of Deaf sport opportunities that can guide their children's involvement through the various levels of participation. Ellis (2001) found that Deaf children with two Deaf parents were more physically active than Deaf children who had at least one hearing parent. It is possible that in the study Deaf parents were more aware of their children's capabilities and opportunities to participate. While this study exerted the impact of Deaf parents on their Deaf children's cultural and deafness-specific activity involvement, most Deaf children are likely to be introduced to Deaf sport by a hearing individual, given that approximately 10 percent of Deaf children have deaf parents (Marschark, 1997; Moores, 2001).

Coaches and physical education teachers play a critical role in introducing Deaf children to Deaf sport (Stewart, Robinson, & McCarthy, 1991; Stewart & Ellis, 1999). A critical factor in Deaf students' social and psychological well-being and success in school was their identification with the Deaf community and the potential of interaction and socialization with others with similar means of communication and experiences (Vialle & Paterson, 1998). "Within schools, a focus on Deaf sport and various Deaf cultural activities is a convenient vehicle for orienting deaf students to the beliefs and actions of the Deaf community. The activities of Deaf sport tend to occur more frequently than other cultural activities and therefore are more readily accessible" (Stewart, 1991, p. 186).

Deaf Sport as a Social Paradigm

The most prominent dimension of Deaf sport is its social sphere, which thrives in an environment that relies on signing for communication. Hence, a primary function of sporting events for Deaf people is as a catalyst for the socialization of a low-incidence and geographically dispersed population (Stewart, 1991).

Deaf sport provides an environment where competition relies solely on athletic prowess because communication equality has been attained. In fact, the motto of the Deaflympics is *Equal through sports* and encompasses an experience in which actual competition makes up only a small part of Deaf sport. Deaf sport is a true extension of Deaf culture.

In the hearing world, very few instances for meaningful socialization through precise communication are available for a Deaf person. This is similar to instances in which individuals from foreign countries are living and working where their primary language is in the linguistic minority (Foster, 1998; Parasnis, 2000). Such barriers tend to be frustrating and in some cases lead to social isolation of the Deaf individual (Bain, Scott, Steinberg, 2004; Stinson & Whitmire, 1996). In fact, Deaf sport promotes social and communicative enrichment among individuals who function in a hearing society that imposes social isolation, low self-image, and a sense of being ostracized for being "different" (Stewart, 1991). Deaf sport

Etiquette When Meeting Someone Who Is Deaf

Do not be surprised if a Deaf person uses words differently. You need to remember English is their second language. When you communicate with a Deaf person without an interpreter, the communication needs to be short and straightforward. Do not exaggerate or overpronounce words. It might cause confusion when the person is trying to understand what is being said. The following are some recommendations that might enhance the communication with a deaf person:

- Use shorter sentences.
- Look directly at a Deaf person when you are speaking.
- Maintain eye contact with the Deaf person even if the interpreter is with you.
- When speaking to a Deaf person, avoid covering your mouth.
- Get the person's attention before you begin to communicate. You would want to get a Deaf person's attention by calling out his or her name. If that fails, a tap on the shoulder or another visual signal such as a hand wave will work.
- If using an interpreter, avoid saying, "Does she understand me?" You need to talk to the Deaf person directly, use the interpreter, and say, "Do you understand me?"
- If you do not understand a Deaf person, do not pretend you do. Patience is essential when speaking and listening to a Deaf person.
- If there is an interpreter with you, you need to wait and give the interpreter time to finish before you ask questions. The interpreter is a few words behind. Please allow time for the Deaf person to look at a paper if you distribute it. A deaf person cannot look at the paper and watch the interpreter at the same time.

in and of itself espouses a sense of belonging and acceptance, something not readily available in many settings.

For many successful Deaf people, Deaf sport provides an early forum for socialization, which may become the ultimate building block for interaction with others, both hearing and deaf, from diverse backgrounds, cultures, and communication preferences. In a world where spoken communication is at a premium, the socialization aspect of Deaf sport provides a much-needed respite from the linguistic communication among colleagues and friends alike, granting a base of common understanding through socialization among individuals sharing similar experiences. The importance of socialization in Deaf sport has been discussed as one of the most essential reasons many Deaf individuals become and stay involved. Many touch on the dramatic difference between communication and socialization in their daily lives and communication and socialization in Deaf sport. Deaf people clearly understand these obstacles in the hearing world. At the same time, the growth and success generated by the forum of Deaf sport could very well lead to greater success and enjoyment in the hearing world.

two
dos

Learning About Hispanic Culture

The story of Hispanics in America is the story of America itself. The Hispanic community's values—love of family, a deep and abiding faith, and a strong work ethic—are America's values. They have enriched our culture and brought creativity and innovation to everything from sports to the sciences and from the arts to our economy (Obama, B., 2010).

This statement was part of President Obama's speech during the proclamation of National Hispanic Heritage Month in 2010. People of Latin American origin are commonly referred to as Hispanic or Latino. But are they Hispanic or Latino? This is a continual debate whose answer, in general terms, depends more on a personal preference than anything else. The term Hispanic is used in all government forms and refers to a race, while Latino refers to a nationality, that of a Latin American country (see figure 2.1). However, there is no real consensus about the use of the word. To some, the term Hispanic is connected to Spain, while Latino is related to a Latin American country. However, most Hispanics or Latinos prefer that people refer to them using their country of origin: Mexican, Puerto Rican, Cuban, and so on.

Some people are adamant about being called Hispanic, others Latinos; there are still others for whom the term does not make a difference. Since there is no real consensus, from this point onward in the text, we use the term Hispanic. The Hispanic population is not only increasing in number and percentage in the United States, but as mentioned before, more and more Hispanics are involved in society as well as the school environment. While it would be very useful for teachers of English-speaking students to learn some of the Spanish language in order to reap its many benefits, such as enhanced communication, it is not enough. It is also important for teachers and students to learn about the culture and its influence on society.

Figure 2.1 Map of Latin American countries.

Why should learning about Hispanic culture and Spanish language be important in schools? If the Hispanic population is increasing everywhere in the United States and we see more and more Spanish-speaking students in schools, what can teachers do? Where does the Hispanic culture fit in?

These are some of the very valid questions that all teachers face today. For a long time, the Spanish language and its culture have been part of what today is known as the United States. In fact, Spanish was spoken on the continent even before English. The first European settlers in the United States were Spaniards. They settled in many places throughout the United States and all throughout the

American continent, including Mexico. Mexico gained its independence from Spain in 1810. The Mexican-American War was driven by the idea of Manifest Destiny, which involved Americans who wanted to expand their territory from the Atlantic to the Pacific coasts. The war ended when the United States defeated the Mexican army, which resulted in the annexation of Texas, California, New Mexico, Arizona, Nevada, Utah, and parts of Colorado and Wyoming to the United States. Consequently, many Mexicans migrated to the United States with their families, language, and culture, which have become an integral part of what the United States is today.

Today, many Hispanics come to this country in search of a better life, looking for the land of opportunity. According to the U.S. Census Bureau (2009), the Hispanic population in the United States has grown from 9.6 million in 1970 to a projected 47.8 million in 2010. That is a change from 4.7 percent to a projected 15.5 percent of the U.S. population by the year 2010. The biggest concentration of Hispanics is in the states of California, Texas, Florida, New York, and Illinois, respectively. The number of Hispanic family households by 2008 was 10.4 million, and 62 percent of them included children younger than 18 years.

Sport and Its Relationship to Hispanic Culture

Physical education teachers need to find strategies to help Hispanic students to succeed in sports while overcoming language and cultural barriers in order to fully emerge in school and ultimately integrate into their new society (Gay & Howard, 2000). Because there are increasing numbers of Hispanic students attending schools in the United States, teachers—even when they get help from English as a second language (ESL) programs—are faced with the need to integrate these students into their regular teaching and help them participate in physical education.

While the ideal situation is to have physical education teachers who are bilingual, we realize that that is not the case, nor can we expect to force physical education teachers to be fluent in the Spanish language. One way to ameliorate the situation and enhance the communication is for physical education teachers to become familiar with common Spanish vocabulary and correct pronunciation. Speaking some words in Spanish can make a child who is Hispanic feel included and valued in the physical education class.

Results from several studies have indicated that minority children do not engage in the recommended 60 minutes of physical activity per day. Among these minority groups, 19 percent were Hispanic children, and they were classified as overweight (Burton & VanHeest, 2007). Unfortunately, lack of participation in physical activity is more evident in Hispanic females because of their typical role in their culture, where they are raised to take care of their families and the household chores. Also, the lack of access to recreation and sport facilities in many neighborhoods reduces the opportunities to engage in any physical activity or sport. As a result, physical education teachers are faced with the great responsibility of satisfying the needs of a growing population and reducing the barriers. To satisfy those needs, it is important to eliminate the language barriers. Physical education teachers and coaches could have a great impact on their students' lifestyles if the communication is effective.

Sports play an important role in the Hispanic culture. As direct participants, as spectators, and as part of support systems and services, Hispanics in the United States have a considerable tradition of participation. According to the adjusted 2000 Census Report and Economic Census Data, Hispanics contribute hundreds of millions of dollars and billions of hours to sporting activities, sport-related employment, and spectator sport recreation.

Studies indicate that Hispanic students may find that participation in sport creates opportunities for acceptance within the majority culture of the school. On the other hand, other Hispanic youths reject school sport as a symbol of their feelings of estrangement from that same culture. Immigrant youth from any country may find participation in school sport especially difficult because of language problems, lack of economic resources, and unfamiliarity with traditional U.S. sports, such as football (McGehee, 2004). Once again, the language barriers often factor into the decision to be physically active.

Even though there are language barriers, many Hispanics have turned into sport heroes in the United States. For example, more than 25 percent of Major League Baseball (MLB) players are from Latin America. Nine of them were inducted into the Major League Baseball Hall of Fame; Roberto Clemente from Puerto Rico was the first. He died in a plane accident while flying to Nicaragua to transport supplies for earthquake victims in 1972. Role models in sport are instrumental for all children, including those who are Hispanic. These role models can be featured in the school environment on bulletin boards, in presentations, in units, or in visual aids.

Hispanic Role Models in Sport

Hispanics excel in almost every sport in the United States—not just in baseball, but also in sports such as figure skating, wrestling, martial arts, and soccer. Following are some of the most prominent Hispanic athletes who serve as role models.

Baseball (MLB)

Albert Pujols, Dominican Republic

Roberto Clemente, Puerto Rico

Juan Antonio Marichal, Dominican Republic

Bernie Williams, Puerto Rico

Tony Pérez, Cuba

Nomar Garcíaparra, Mexico

Sandy Alomar, Puerto Rico

Jorge Posada, Puerto Rico

Roberto Alomar, Puerto Rico

Basketball (NBA and WNBA)

Rolando Blackman, Panamá

Rebecca Lobo, Cuba

Carmelo Anthony, Puerto Rico

Carlos Arroyo, Puerto Rico

José Juan Barea, Puerto Rico

Courtesy of Barbara Moore.

Albert Pujols, who serves as a role model to people all over the world, is one of the most prominent Hispanic athletes in Major League Baseball.

Manu Ginóbili, Argentina

Luis Scola, Argentina

Esteban Batista, Uruguay

Boxing

Julio César Chávez, Mexico

Oscar de la Hoya, Mexico

Miguel Cotto, Puerto Rico

Félix Trinidad, Puerto Rico

Juan Manuel López, Puerto Rico

Robert Guerrero, Mexico

Delia González, Mexico

David Obregón, Nicaragua

Football (NFL)

Tony Romo, Mexico

Tom Fears, Mexico

Anthony Muñoz, Mexico

Mark Sánchez, Mexico

Golf (PGA and LPGA)

Chi Chi Rodríguez, Puerto Rico

Nancy López, Mexico

Lee Treviño, Mexico

Camilo Villegas, Colombia

Lorena Ochoa, Mexico

Soccer

Diego Maradona, Argentina

Esteban Arias, Mexico

Marcelo Balboa, Argentina

Chris Armas, Puerto Rico

Cuauhtemoc Blanco, Mexico

Carlos Bocanegra, Mexico

Diego Gutierrez, Colombia

Orlando Pérez, Puerto Rico

Tab Ramos, Uruguay

Wrestling

Eddie Guerrero, Mexico

Enrique Torres, Mexico

Tito Santana, Mexico

Eve Torres, Nicaragua

Lilian García, Spain and Puerto Rico

Candice Michelle, Costa Rica

Chavo Guerrero Jr., Mexico

Other Sports

Tony Alba, skateboarding, Mexico

Stacey Peralta, skateboarding, Mexico

Derek Parra, speed skating, Mexico

Gigi Fernández, tennis, Puerto Rico

Rafael Nadal, tennis, Spain

Lisa Fernández, softball, Cuba and Puerto Rico

Javier Gaspar, volleyball, Puerto Rico

Natasha Sagardía, surfing, Puerto Rico

Juan Pablo Montoya, car racing, Colombia

Helio Castroneves, car racing, Brazil

part II

Importance of Infusing Language Into Physical Activity Programs

Part II provides innovative ideas on integrating a different language into physical activity settings. Note that although we use Spanish and sign language as examples in this book, any spoken or visual language can be infused into physical education with the use of the techniques that are suggested here. Learning languages other than English is important to the growth of all students. To ensure that learning is taking place, you have the option of assessing your students.

Chapter 3 offers strategies for teaching in a K-12 setting and also offers ideas that university professors can use for infusing language into courses. Chapter 4 offers various strategies for assessing students in learning of receptive and productive language in physical education classes. Assessment can be formative in nature (meaning that it is conducted during the activities) or summative (conducted at the end of a unit or activity).

Chapters 5, 6, and 7 present activities and strategies that can be used for students in elementary through high school. Strategies that can be used in higher education settings are also presented. By incorporating these activities in your lesson plans, you will be able to demonstrate culturally responsive pedagogical strategies to your students.

three
tres

Infusing Language Into Physical Education

The choice to infuse language into teaching is made by teachers in order to accommodate students who may speak a different language and to increase knowledge about culture and language by itself. Once students learn some basic language, the benefits to the students, teachers, and community are endless. This chapter presents strategies that you can use when teaching language to students in your PE classes. While there are very specific language teaching strategies that you can learn, there is also intuitive knowledge that most adults use with younger children when trying to communicate with them. This kind of speech that an adult uses is known as "motherese," "caretaker speech," "teacherese," or "foreigner talk." According to Bruner (1983), when an adult is talking to a child, the adult tends to use shorter, less complex sentences; checks the meaning with the child frequently to make sure the child understands; uses more concrete referents; and uses gestures and visual reinforcement.

DVD Some of the Spanish words presented in chapter 8 might be difficult to pronounce. If this is the case, you can refer to the Spanish pronunciation videos on the DVD, or you can seek help from a student or a colleague who speaks or understands Spanish. Regional dialects do exist among Hispanic groups; therefore, clarification might be necessary in many cases. It might be useful to have a variety of words in Spanish for the same term.

Strategies for Teachers in Elementary and Secondary Education

The possibility for collaboration between the Spanish teacher and you (the physical education teacher) may be present if students are learning a second language already, such as Spanish. This collaboration reinforces and applies what is being taught in the Spanish class into the physical education class. The same can be true for any language taught at the school (Lieberman, Columna, Martínez de la Vega Mansilla, & Taylor, 2010).

In chapter 8, words frequently used in physical education are listed in alphabetical order, and their Spanish translations are included. In chapter 9, lists of PE words are listed by themes, and their American signs are included. Organizing the words either by alphabetical order or by theme can assist you in providing students with a repertoire of words. You can select your preferred format for sharing these words with students. Following are general strategies that you can use while infusing Spanish or sign language into your classroom:

- Use gestures and visual reinforcements.
- Use instructional aids (pictures, flash cards, visual aids; see figure 3.1).
- Seek support from those students who speak Spanish or use sign language. You can give them the lesson plan and meet with them outside the physical education time to discuss what words you want to incorporate into your class.
- Scaffold the activities. That is, organize the activities in such a way that, with the knowledge the students have and your input, they will be able to complete the task at hand.

Figure 3.1 Spanish words and sign language are integrated into this playground infusing language into the play of visiting children.

- **DVD** On the DVD, refer to the videos of Spanish pronunciations and sign language frequently used by teachers in physical education settings.
- Find websites that translate movement- and sport-related words from English to Spanish (and signs) and that include audio clips of their pronunciations. You can also provide students with websites that they can visit on their own and practice signs or Spanish words while at home.
- Have daily words or signs that the students and you can learn (i.e., have a word of the day). The assignment should be relevant to the course content.
- Learn and post basic sign language or Spanish, such as *bathroom*, *stop*, *hurt*, and *water*.
- Be able to provide cues in sign language or Spanish, such as *low*, *high*, *short*, *long*, *hard*, and *soft*.
- Learn positive words and formulaic expressions in sign language or Spanish (e.g., *great*, *good job*, *way to go*). This might help in providing feedback to the students.
- Give words as homework to students so they can take the words (e.g., sport or skill terminology) and practice them at home with their parents. It is best that you teach one category at a time. For instance, if you plan to teach students an activity that involves colors, you would want to teach them signs about colors. This way, students are more likely to retain the information.
- Create a sign language or Spanish club after school and teach more signs or Spanish to those students who are interested.
- Divide the class into small groups. If bilingual students are available, assign one bilingual student to each group. That student can serve as a translator for the rest of the group. The activities can be presented in either Spanish or English, and students need to follow the instructions. This type of group activity might promote socialization among the students. Note that the groups should rotate so that Hispanic students have the opportunity to interact with other students in class.

Remember that infusing a foreign language into the curriculum requires planning and commitment from you. Following are strategies for infusing only Spanish in the curriculum:

- Speak the language slowly, but don't exaggerate.
- Articulate clearly and use distinct pronunciations.
- Use short, noncomplex sentences.
- Rephrase things and repeat.
- Frequently check for understanding.
- Emphasize communication among the students (e.g., ¿Cuantos años tienes?, ¿Cuál es tu juego favorito? [How old are you? Which is your favorite game?]).
- Use as many concrete examples and demonstrations as possible.

Another strategy that you can use in learning and teaching Spanish to classes is organizing a Hispanic Game Day. Assign a specific Spanish-speaking country to be represented that day. The students need to look for games, clothing, traditions, food, and any other characteristic of that country and have a day dedicated to the culture of the selected country. Have a map of the country with key facts in Spanish and English. Ask parents, especially Hispanic parents, for help. Although there is much enthusiasm related to infusing Spanish into physical education, you should know that there are some misconceptions about children who speak Spanish and are learning English.

Following are strategies that you can use when infusing only sign language into your physical education programs. When you are teaching American Sign Language (ASL), you are giving the students a skill that will be useful to them. It is fun to teach ASL to your classes, and it does not require using any equipment. From our experience, students enjoy learning ASL.

- When teaching ASL to a hearing group, it may be appropriate to begin with a "what if?" scenario. You could say, "If you go to a foreign country and you do not speak their language, how will you communicate with them?" This is a good way to start a conversation that helps students learn about the Deaf culture.
- Ask the students to think about how their lives would be if they could not hear.
- Remind students that deaf people do not see themselves as disabled.
- Sign language often moves quickly. Students will remember words and phrases easily if they are presented in a context. An example would be students learning their colors while playing a parachute game related to colors. Another example might be students learning of places in their neighborhood while playing a "treasure hunt" around their neighborhood. Once students have learned how to sign the selected words, you can incorporate those words into games or activities.
- It is ideal for students *not* to use their voices. If they do not rely on speaking, students will be able to pick up signs more quickly. For example, teach a simple game with signs and gestures, such as a tag game using colors or animals (see chapter 5 for elementary games).

Most students love taking physical education class regardless of their race, sex, or ability. For them, entering the gym means entering a world of movement activities, challenges, and opportunities to be successful. These things are possible if you create a safe and positive learning environment for all students. You can use practically any game to learn Spanish or sign language. You just need to use some creativity to make modifications. For example, you can have a variation of the game Pictionary in which there are as many teams as you decide. One student on each team uses a predetermined locomotor skill to get to a certain place where there are flash cards with action words in Spanish or ASL signs. The student then comes back and performs the action (written on the card) in front of his team. The team needs to say the word in Spanish or make the ASL sign in order to score. This focuses on the locomotor skills as well as the language.

The assistance of a language teacher may be helpful for the physical education teacher to acquire words in any given language. According to Estrada, Gómez, and Ruiz-Escalante (2009), there are four misconceptions about teaching English language learners:

1. *The most effective way to ensure that students learn English is to immerse them in English.* Studies have shown that the most effective way is to teach students in both their first language and in their second language.

2. *Through immersion, they will learn enough English within a year to survive academically.* English language learners need five to seven years to master English well enough to work proficiently.

3. *Once the students have achieved oral fluency in English, they are capable of academic learning in mainstream English-only classrooms.* Grade-level cognitive proficiency in language is achieved through a student's first language.

4. *The less the students use their first language, the better.* The more the students use their native language in school, building as many skills as they can in that language, the better. In other words, the most effective way to teach and meet the needs of Hispanic students is through an English–Spanish program.

Another benefit of teaching in both languages is that the teacher and the non-Spanish-speaking students acquire proficiency in a second language.

You should acknowledge, appreciate, and respect diversity among students and plan your physical education classes accordingly. McCollum, Civalier, and Holt (2004) suggest some strategies that you can use when teaching Hispanic students in your class:

- Use instructional strategies that foster social interactions (e.g., peer teaching and cooperative games).
- Use a buddy system (pair a Hispanic student with a non-Hispanic student).
- Use visual demonstrations along with verbal explanation of tasks.
- Include activities that have a Hispanic origin when relevant to lesson objectives. For example, when using music for Go and Stop, use Latin rhythms or music with Spanish lyrics (see chapter 5 for elementary games and chapter 7 for high school games).
- Post rules in both languages.

Strategies for Instructors of Preservice Students

If you are a physical education curriculum instructor who is teaching preservice students, you can use the following suggestions to help your students in their preparation for teaching a curriculum that incorporates Spanish or sign language.

Inclusion of Spanish or Sign Language in Curriculum

Just as you would do when working with children, it is best to use words in Spanish (or signs in ASL) that are directly related to the content the students are learning, not just as a tidbit of information. You can teach sign language and Spanish words each day to build up the vocabulary of your preservice teachers so that they will be prepared for teaching. The content can include colors, locomotor skills, positive feedback, formations, directions, instructional terms, and numbers. This daily exercise, which presents two or three words per day, can take from 30 seconds to 3 minutes depending on the depth of the words taught and the number of words reviewed each day (Lieberman et al., 2010). This practice enriches the curriculum, allowing students to learn the words or formulaic expressions that they most commonly use in teaching physical education.

By observing your students' practicum experience or their use of productive and receptive language, you can assess students' proficiency in the words taught or in the use of productive and receptive language on a quiz or test. Following is an example of a quiz question: You (the professor) sign in ASL or say a word in Spanish; the students write the word in English in the blank space on the quiz. Professors can set this up at any level of difficulty considering the proficiency of their students. Here is one question many professors ask themselves when trying to infuse Spanish and sign language in classes: Should Spanish and sign language be taught at the same time or individually? The answer to this question depends on the goals of the class and the comfort level of the professor (Lieberman et al., 2010). It is possible to teach both at the same time, such as teaching colors in Spanish and in sign language during the same week. Research results indicate that the acquisition of academic skills is not impaired when students have a double-immersion program (a program in which students are taught two second languages at the same time, a common practice that has great success in several countries) (Cenoz & Genesee, 1998). Many times the Spanish will reinforce the signs and vice versa. In addition, some students may be visual learners and pick up the sign language very quickly.

Use of Websites

As a professor, you can provide preservice teachers with lists of Spanish and sign language websites, which can help the students prepare language teaching. You could also provide students with common formulaic expressions or words they can use during peer teaching or during their practicum. ASL and Spanish websites are listed in two tables in appendix A. A brief description of each website is included. These websites are a great resource that professors, teachers, and student teachers can use when planning courses.

Foreign Language Requirements for Teacher Candidates

Professional preparation programs should require students to gain proficiency in a foreign language before they graduate. Many four-year colleges require students to take two or four semesters of a foreign language. The physical education or kinesiology departments and language departments may collaborate, and a course could be taught that uses common terms in physical education classes (Lieberman et al., 2010). Note that it is impossible to take courses that relate to every language that students will encounter, but future teachers need to consider their personal interests and the most predominant language in the geographical area in which they want to teach. For example, if a future teacher plans on teaching in California, she should consider learning Spanish, but if she were to obtain employment in certain areas of Columbus, Ohio, she might benefit from learning Somali.

With some time, energy, and effort teachers can infuse language into their classes. The sensitivity and the way in which this information is delivered can make a significant impact upon the students in class. Done correctly students will have a greater knowledge of the languages and cultures that are an integral part of their community.

four
cuatro

Assessing Learning

> A child develops language at their own pace and within their own contexts, and documentation allows educators to discover a child's individual language development (Vakil, Freeman, & Swim, 2003, p. 301).

Students love to learn language, and physical education class is an excellent setting for acquiring a second language. Effective teaching can be determined through assessment, which takes thoughtful planning, creativity, and time. The satisfaction of knowing your students are learning everything you are teaching is an outcome of good assessment. Assessing language acquisition effectively in physical education will motivate students to learn more and enjoy the process at the same time.

This chapter reviews a few approaches and offers a variety of ways of identifying whether your approach to teaching language is working or if you need to change your approach. The focus here is on assessing words learned in Spanish or sign language.

State standards for physical education and the standards of the National Association for Sport and Physical Education (NASPE) do not include language acquisition skills as part of their requirements. If you choose to infuse language into your daily lessons, know that you are a culturally responsive teacher. You might also want to spend time assessing your students' language acquisition in each unit throughout the year.

Determining the Purpose of the Assessment

Language experts believe that teachers should provide students with opportunities to demonstrate knowledge in nontraditional ways (O'Malley & Valdez Pierce, 1996). For example, a class is given the Spanish word *playa* (which means *beach*), and they have to perform a movement that they would do at the beach (like swimming, volleyball, playing Frisbee, or building a sand castle). Assessment of words presented in class should be conducted through the use of authentic material that connects with students' experiences in their personal and academic contexts (Davis Lensky, Ehlers-Zavala, Daniel, & Sun-Irminger, 2006).

Assessment can be used to determine teaching effectiveness, understanding of language, and grades. When you know the purpose of the assessment, you will have a better idea of how to implement the use of different languages in your class.

1. Teaching effectiveness can be assessed in a variety of ways. In an authentic assessment during the lesson, you would determine children's understanding of some basic concepts, such as *rápido* (fast) and *lento* (slow) by playing a tag game and determining if the child moves faster or slower when you tell them to in Spanish. It is important to assess using a variety of methods so you really find out what the students know and in what areas they need assistance. Examples are self-assessment and the use of rubrics to determine words learned or content taught. (Both are discussed in the following section.)

2. Regarding understanding of language, you might just want to determine whether the students know the words that were taught in a specific unit, such as colors, numbers, formations, letters, and movement patterns.

3. Regarding grades, you might want to embed language into your grading system. For example, teachers can assign a grade for language as part of their cognitive assessment. In this case the assessment must be objective, meaning that the grading system must be clearly defined.

Remember that you must assess achievement only in the words and units you have taught. It is also important to assess students during or shortly after the completion of a unit so the information is fresh in their minds. Assessment later in the year on concepts presented earlier will determine the level of learning and retention of the words learned, which is important as well.

Examples of Assessing Learning of Language

There are many ways that you can assess words learned in various units. Two simple ways are self-assessment and the use of rubrics. Self-assessment encourages learners to become actively involved in monitoring their own progress (Davis Lensky et al., 2006). Self-assessment encourages students to identify successful behaviors, in this case which words they have mastered and which ones they have not. Self-assessment can be done with lists of words that students learn, rubrics (e.g., I understand this word all of the time, most of the time, sometimes, or never), or photos of the skills (students write down the Spanish word or sign the word when they see the photo).

With the use of rubrics (also known as checklists), you can identify aspects of an assignment or activity that are most important and assign relative point values to each component. When a student uses self-assessment, he is assessing his perception of his ability to use the language. You should use self-assessment formatively (i.e., during the activity) to gain information about the language competence of the students. If the students are weak in specific areas, then you can review those areas, use more visuals, repeat the information more often, or use the areas that need improvement in a variety of contexts to assist the most learners.

The checklists in figure 4.1 are two examples of self-assessment that could be used for both Spanish and sign language. **DVD** You can use these checklists to assess students' understanding of the basic concepts of the lesson.

Spanish Rubric for Parachute		
Colors to learn: red, yellow, blue, green, orange, purple	Yes	No
5: I know all of the colors of the parachute.		
4: I know five of the colors of the parachute.		
3: I know four of the colors of the parachute.		
2: I know three of the colors of the parachute.		
1: I know two of the colors of the parachute.		
Sign Language Rubric for Object Control Skills		
Object control words: catch, throw, kick, bat, roll a ball	Yes	No
5: I know all of the object control words.		
4: I know four of the object control words.		
3: I know three of the object control words.		
2: I know two of the object control words.		
1: I know one of the object control words.		

Figure 4.1 Two examples of self-assessment to use when infusing Spanish and sign language into physical education classes.

From L. Columna and L. Lieberman, 2011, *Promoting Language Through Physical Education* (Champaign, IL: Human Kinetics).

Understanding Language

To assess students' understanding of the language, you can do a variety of things:

1. Give the whole class an instruction in the language you want to assess and see who executes the skill appropriately.
2. Use peer or self-assessment with rubrics.
3. Have small groups of students lead activities, such as stretches or small games, in the language you are assessing.

The following are examples of ways to use assessments that can be incorporated in classes in order to assess the words learned by a given group of students.

1. Whole-class assessment can be done in an authentic way on your command. You can ask the class to slide to the right in Spanish (a la derecha) and determine how many students understood the command when it was given and who had to look around for clarification. In another example, using basketball skills, you can determine whether the students understand numbers and the command for the pair, such as shoot or dribble. In addition, you can combine the numbers and psychomotor commands to assess comprehension of each.

2. Peers can assess the receptive language of one another with the use of rubrics similar to those provided earlier. This way they are also working on receptive and productive language. The rubrics can be simple like the previous ones or they can be more like sport-related checklists, such as the one in figure 4.2 related to baseball. **DVD**

3. Divide the class into groups of four or five. One student leads activities such as stretches or small games in the language you taught and want to assess. Then paraeducators or aides can help in the assessment of language in the same way the peers assess. The paraeducator can use the checklists or the rubrics with any child in the class.

Peer Checklist for Baseball Signs

Place a check mark next to the words that your partner knows in sign language. Your partner must be able to use the word correctly two times before he or she gets a check. The partner says a word in English or signs the word to you. Then you either sign or say in Spanish the words back to the partner.

_____Bat	_____Home run	_____Captain
_____First base	_____Short stop	_____Team
_____Second base	_____Pitcher	_____Win
_____Third base	_____Third inning	_____Lose
_____Home plate	_____Coach	

Figure 4.2 An example of a peer-assessment checklist to use when infusing Spanish and sign language into physical education classes.

From L. Columna and L. Lieberman, 2011, *Promoting Language Through Physical Education* (Champaign, IL: Human Kinetics).

The peer assessments can be used in the middle or the end of a unit depending on how you want to use the information. The small-group assessment can also be used at the middle or at the end of each unit. Small groups can also be used for the purpose of assessing student learning. In this approach, have students lead activities, such as stretches or small games, in the language you are assessing. You will find out the words they are proficient in as well as the ones they need some help on. An example is to divide a class of 32 into 4 groups of 8 students. Allow two volunteers to give their group commands, such as "jump to the elephant." They will then jump to the elephant on the wall individually or in pairs. You can see what the leaders know and also see if the class understands their commands.

Leaders can also instruct the group in stretches by signing or saying the Spanish words of the body parts that are being stretched, such as *brazo* (arm) or *cabeza* (head). These activities are fun as well as useful in your assessment of the students' language skills.

Grades

You can determine grades with the use of informal techniques explained previously as well as on written tests. Receptive understanding can be assessed with the use of a written test: You can sign or say a word or phrase in Spanish and the students can write down the word in English or vice-versa. You can assess productive language in a small group by asking each student a word in English or in sign language and then determining whether they know the word individually by their answer. For example the teacher may say in English the word "red", and the student should sign or say in Spanish the word "rojo". In some cases, students might not know the word out of context, so it might be helpful if you act out the word. For example, if you are testing words related to a swimming unit, saying the word *dive* or showing a dive might help them remember the Spanish word or the sign.

five
cinco

Elementary School Activities

The activities in this section focus on fundamental movements, object control, locomotor skills, and basic concepts. Children of this age must develop a foundation of movement and motor skills. These dynamic games and activities involve movement concepts as well as the word concepts of numbers, colors, animals, the alphabet, and directions. Every game in this book can be used with sign language or Spanish unless otherwise noted.

Note that you should practice beforehand the words that you want to incorporate in the lessons so that you can instruct smoothly and clearly. Also, using visual and auditory input during instruction will ensure that children have a multisensory approach to learning sign language or Spanish or whatever language you choose to incorporate.

Photo courtesy of William Turk.

Students enjoy jumping during a locomotor game using sign language, and the student teacher picked up very quickly on the signing used.

Balance Tag

This is a great warm-up activity to get students moving and to increase their heart rates.

Words Learned

- Head (cabeza)
- Hand (mano)
- Foot (pie)
- Shoulder (hombro)
- Knee (rodilla)
- Toes (dedos de los pies)
- Fingers (dedos de las manos)
- Nose (nariz)
- Arm (brazo)

Equipment Needed

1 beanbag per student

Description

To begin, each student has a beanbag and a partner. Partners must decide who is the It player (this can easily be done by who wins a quick game of rock-paper-scissors). When you say to begin, It must try to tag his partner after spinning around in one spot for two full rotations. When you call out a body part in Spanish, students who are not It must balance the beanbag on that body part while trying to tag their partner. The students' ability level and age will determine what body parts they are capable of balancing the beanbag on. If the beanbag falls off of It, he must pick up the beanbag and place it on his body before he can continue tagging. If the non-It partner loses the beanbag, she must pick up the beanbag and tell It, and they will then switch roles (the non-It player will become It).

Variations

Change the equipment to make the tasks more challenging or easier. For example, students can balance a wand or a block. Change the body parts on which the students balance their beanbags. For example, students can balance the object on the right or left knee. Maximize or minimize the playing area to increase or decrease the number of students per area. Students can do other movements, such as jumping jacks, tuck jumps, or balancing for five seconds, before trying to tag the partner.

Parachute Play (Jugando con el Paracaídas)

In this game the parachute is used as a medium for facilitating locomotor skills, colors, numbers, and directionality.

Words Learned

- Red (rojo)
- Yellow (amarillo)
- Green (verde)
- Bear (oso)
- Jump (saltar, salta [s.], salten [pl.])
- Frog (sapo or rana)

Equipment Needed

Parachute

Description

The class members gather around the parachute. You sign and say in Spanish a color and a skill. When you sign yellow (amarillo) and bear (oso), the students who are on that color will walk like a bear under the parachute. If they are on green (verde), they will jump (saltar, salta [s.], salten [pl.]) like a frog (sapo or rana).

Note: Whenever you give a command, you will need to conjugate the verbs into the command form. A command will be in either the singular command form or the plural command form, depending on whether you are talking to one student or to several students at a time. For example, the infinitive for jump in Spanish is saltar. The informal singular command (for one student) is salta and the command form for several students (plural) is salten. In the vocabulary lists in this text, the command forms for both singular and plural, respectively, appear next to the infinitive. The (s.) symbolizes the singular form while (pl.) means plural.

Variations

You can change the concepts. For example, walk (caminar, camina [s.], caminen [pl.]) to the right (derecha) and to the left (izquierda), and do so at different levels: high (alto), medium (mediano), low (bajo).

Red Light Green Light (Luz Roja Luz Verde) (Spanish Only)

In this game, the game of Red Light Green Light is modified using Spanish words.

Words Learned

- Red (rojo)
- Yellow (amarillo)
- Green (verde)
- Blue (azul)

- Start over (volver, vuelve [s.], vuelvan [pl.] a empezar or empezar, empieza [s.], empiecen [pl.] de nuevo)
- Stop (parar, para [s.], paren [pl.])
- Go on (continuar, continúa [s.], continúen [pl.])

Equipment Needed

- Cones
- Poly spots

Description

The caller faces the wall and says, "Verde," which is green, meaning go. The students move toward the caller. When the caller turns around to face the students while simultaneously saying, "Rojo," which means red, the students have to stop. Whoever is still moving after the caller's "Rojo" and turn must go back to the start position. The game is played completely in Spanish so the students learn colors and the words stop and go. Note that this game is not conducive to using sign language because the leader has to face away from the students.

Variations

The students can do locomotor movements according to the color. For example, verde (green) means to jump (brincar), and azul (blue) means to gallop (galopar).

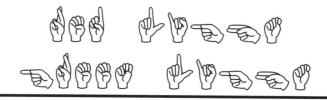

Obstacle Course Mania (Carrera de Obstáculo)

In this game students complete an obstacle course to facilitate the concept of directionality and laterality in both Spanish and sign language.

Words Learned

- Over (por arriba)
- Under (abajo)
- Around (alrededor)
- In (adentro)
- Out (afuera)
- Through (a través de)
- On (en)
- Slow (lento)
- Fast (rápido)
- Cone (cono)

Equipment Needed

- Mats
- Poly spots
- Cones
- Hula hoops
- Ropes
- Bolster

Description

Create an obstacle course using the concepts of adverbs: over, under, around, in, out, through, and on. All of these words are important to know in Spanish or sign language. Students can go through the course in pairs and use the words that describe what their partner is doing (e.g., around cones, over a bolster, under two hula hoops, through a mat).

Variations

Students can perform movements at different speeds. For example, you can tell them to run (correr, corre [s.], corran [pl.]) fast (rápido) around (alrededor) the cone (del cono).

Circus Owner (El Dueño del Circo)

In this game, students practice locomotor skills while performing the movements of various animals.

Words Learned

- Monkeys (monos)
- Giraffes (jirafas)
- Lions (leones)
- Elephants (elefantes)
- Animals (animales)
- Come out (salir, sal [s.], salgan [pl.])

Equipment Needed

None

Description

Students line up on one side of the gym; each person is designated as an animal. The person who is It stands in the middle. This is a very active tag game where It (the circus owner) is trying to get the animals back into the circus before the show starts. The owner is looking for the animals because they have gotten loose, but the owner knows that the animals are not too far from the circus. So he yells out, "Animales, salgan" (animals, come out), and specific animals such as los monos (monkeys), las jirafas (giraffes), and so on. If students are successful, you can modify the activity by changing the ways in which the animals run, and the students will be required to perform such movements to avoid getting captured by the circus owner.

Variations

Set some stations as cages where a student has to go if he gets tagged by the circus owner until one animal of the same kind untags him. For example, there is a cage for the monkeys. If a monkey is tagged by the circus owner, then the monkey has to go to his cage moving like a monkey and stay there until another monkey untags him.

Capturing Tails (Capturando las Colas)

This is a type of tag game in which students learn colors, locomotor skills, start signals, and stop signals.

Words Learned

- Red (rojo)
- Yellow (amarillo)
- Green (verde)
- Blue (azul)

Equipment Needed

- Flags
- Radio or CD player
- Music

Description

In this activity, students perform a given locomotor skill while the music is playing. Distribute various-colored flags (tails) to students. Students wear the flags as tails with Velcro on them, or they can tuck the flags into their pants. Once the music stops playing, call out a color; any person who is wearing that color is required to prevent his or her flag from being taken away by the other colors. The person whose flag is taken runs to a bucket and gets another flag. At the end, the person or team who has captured the most flags from other players wins.

Variations

Teams can play this game.

Adventure After School (La Aventura Después de la Clase)

In this game students learn locomotor skills, object control, and places in Spanish or sign language.

Words Learned

- Run (correr, corre [s.], corran [pl.])
- Walk (caminar, camina [s.], caminen [pl.])
- Play (jugar, juegan [s.], jueguen [pl.])
- Basketball (baloncesto)
- Soccer (fútbol, balompié)
- Jump rope (saltar, salta [s.], salten [pl.] cuerda)
- Dribble (driblear, driblea [s.], dribleen [pl.])
- Catch (atrapar, atrapa [s.], atrapen [pl.])
- Church (iglesia)
- Park (parque)
- School building (escuela)
- School day (día de clase)
- Beach (playa)
- Ball (pelota, balón)

Equipment Needed

Basketballs, soccer balls, tennis balls, pictures of settings labeled with Spanish terms (e.g., park, mountains, school, beach, church)

Description

Pictures of places such as a beach, church, school, and mountain will be taped all around the gym. In this game, children go on an adventure that takes place after school. They will be handed a card that has a set of instructions on it in Spanish or sign language. They will then go and do what the set of instructions say. For example, a card could say, "Corre (pl. corran) a la casa de un amigo y pasa (pl. pasen) la pelota de baloncesto" (run to a friend's house and pass the basketball). Then, they move to the picture of the place on the card—in this case they will run to the friend's house.

- Once they have arrived at the picture of a house, there will be options for different activi-dades (activities) that the students can do while they are there. Students will randomly select one activity from a pile and complete the activity. Some activities require working with a partner, and some activities can be done alone. For example, they may be at a friend's house and they choose a card that says, "Saltar cuerda" (jump rope) or "Driblear un balón" (dribble a ball) or a sign for run.
- Once they have completed the activity, there will be a card telling them where to go next and how to get there. They will complete the process until they arrive home for dinner.
- Some options for places to go are the beach, church, school, and mountains. The loco-motor activities can be run, walk, jump, skip, hop, or slide.

Variations

Vary the words learned or the activities based on the lesson. Add places to go, locomotor activi-ties, or activities related to the current unit. Integrate interdisciplinary concepts such as countries or capital cities. You can use other languages, including sign language, for teaching this game.

Language Leader Relay

Partners work together to use locomotor skills and test knowledge of words for colors, animals, or numbers.

Words Learned

- Dog (perro)
- Turtle (tortuga)
- Fish (pescado)
- Cat (gato)
- Horse (caballo)

- Yellow (amarillo)
- Blue (azul)
- Red (rojo)
- Green (verde)
- Orange (naranja/anaranjado)

- 1 (uno)
- 2 (dos)
- 3 (tres)
- 4 (cuatro)
- 5 (cinco)

- 6 (seis)
- 7 (siete)
- 8 (ocho)
- 9 (nueve)
- 10 (diez)

Equipment Needed

Pictures of animals, colors, numbers, or any words that you are using in the game. All of the words that students will learn need to be laminated and taped to the wall. At least three pictures of each word need to be laminated. Place three cones in the center of the gymnasium for the starting point.

Description

Before the beginning of the class, decide if you will have the lesson focus on speaking Spanish or using sign language. Then you will teach the sign language or Spanish for the previously listed terms. Divide the students into groups of three or four depending on the class size. Each group lines up (see figure 5.1). The first person in each line (the leader for that pair) signs an animal, color, or number, and so on to the person behind him or her. That person will then run over to the wall and bring back the picture that was signed. The leader and the runner both return to the end of the line. The next two people in line go. Students must switch positions when they reach the front of the line again. Students sign or say the words that are on the wall.

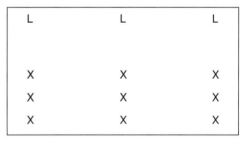

L	L	L
X	X	X
X	X	X
X	X	X

Figure 5.1 Set up for Language Leader Relay.

Variations

Use any theme, preferably themes that were covered in other subject areas such as geography, science, math, or history. For example, have pictures of snow, rain, sun, and clouds; the students can learn words in sign language or Spanish related to weather. Also the objects can be placed around the room. Then the person giving the command will have the entire group of students run to the specific thing that was signed. There should be several pictures of the word mentioned around the room. The next person in line goes and the person who previously gave commands goes to the end of the line. The last variation is that the locomotor movement can change (e.g., from running to skipping).

Shower Hour (La Hora de la Ducha) (Aquatic Activity)

Students use kicking as a medium for learning the words for fast, slow, shower, and kick.

Words Learned

- Kick (patear, patea [s.], pateen [pl.])
- Shower (bañarse, báñate [s.], báñense [pl.])
- Fast (rápido)

Equipment Needed

Swimming pool

Description

Students can hold on to the wall or a flotation device and kick. You can stand near the students and say that you need a good shower with a lot of water: "¡Necesitas (s.)/Necesitan (pl.) tomar un baño con mucha agua!" The students need to kick as hard as possible so that you can "shower" (see figure 5.2).

Figure 5.2 Students try and get the teacher wet by kicking hard in the aquatic activity Shower Hour.

six
seis

Middle School Activities

The activities in this section focus on basic sport and movement concepts. Children at this age must work on the foundation of sport and movement skills. These dynamic games and activities involve movement skills as well as word concepts such as time, fitness, and body parts. Every game in this book can be used with sign language or Spanish unless otherwise noted.

Note that you should practice beforehand the words that you want to incorporate so that you can instruct smoothly and clearly. Also, using visual and auditory input during instruction will ensure that children have a multisensory approach to learning sign language or Spanish or whatever language you choose to incorporate.

Birthday Lineup (Sign Language Only)

Students line up by birthday using only sign language to communicate with one another.

Words Learned

- Hot
- Cold
- Winter
- Spring
- Fall

- Summer
- Yes
- No
- Numbers and alphabet letters

Equipment Needed

None

Description

Students line up in the order of where their birthday falls in the calendar. They are not allowed to speak to anyone while playing the game. Do not give the students any hints; they should be able to figure this out for themselves. Students can use gestures, the alphabet, and numbers. When they are finished, check to see if they are in order. This game is a great icebreaker if you have a Deaf student in your class. This game also motivates the students to learn sign language more quickly. The required sign words are *hot, cold, winter, spring, fall, summer, yes, no,* numbers, and alphabet letters. After the students play the game, you can present this scenario: If you bump into a person who speaks a language different from the one you speak, how can you communicate with that person? A possible answer is by using universal gestures.

Variations

Use the same concept with numbers of siblings, pets, or favorite foods.

Word Play (Juego de Palabras)

Students perform locomotor movements in various locations in the room. The Spanish words and sign language for the location titles are posted around the room.

Words Learned

- Office (oficina)
- Window (ventana)
- Door (puerta)
- Wall (pared)

- Bathroom (baño)
- Basketball (baloncesto)
- Locomotor skills (destrezas locomotoras)

Equipment Needed

Signs around the room

Description

Post labels in Spanish or sign language all over the gymnasium. Label the door, window, office, basketball backboard, bathroom, and so on in Spanish and signs. Give locomotor skills to perform in the various parts of the gym.

Variations

Students can be given locomotor skills to the different various parts of the gym. You can use this as a warm-up at different levels and speeds, which can also be in Spanish or sign language.

Around the World (Alrededor del Mundo)

Students rotate around to various countries throughout the room performing activites related to those countries.

Words Learned

- Run in place (correr, corre [s.], corran [pl.] en el mismo lugar)
- Kick (patear, patea [s.], pateen [pl.])

- 10 times (diez veces)
- 30 seconds (treinta segundos)

Equipment Needed

Varies, depending on the skills that students will be participating in; country die (see description section)

Description

Divide the gym into six stations. Each station is a country in which the primary language is Spanish (e.g., Cuba, Puerto Rico, Venezuela). Write on each side of a die the name of one country. When each student rolls the die, he or she needs to go to that particular station (see figure 6.1). Once students are at their stations, assign several activities for the students to perform. All the activities at each station may be related to a particular skill. For example, in the station of Cuba, the skill to be practiced could be running; the station of Puerto Rico could be kicking. Include instructions in both Spanish and English. For example, the student rolls the die and lands in Cuba. The instructions say to run in place for 30 seconds; the instructions in Spanish would be "Corre (pl. corran) en el mismo lugar por treinta segundos." Another group lands in Puerto Rico. The instruction is to kick the ball 10 times in a row; the instructions in Spanish would be "Patea (pl. pateen) la pelota diez veces consecutivamente." At the end of each station you can ask the meaning of a particular word based on the task that they performed to verify that they learned the words.

Figure 6.1 An example of how you can create a station for students to visit in Around the World.

Variations

The students can search beforehand the most popular sports of those particular countries and do some of the skills when they get to the station. For example, in the station of Argentina, they will dribble a soccer ball for any amount of time, or if the station is Puerto Rico, they will throw a baseball to a target.

Fitness Board Game

While playing this game using a giant board game, students learn Spanish terms for various exercises and activities.

Words Learned

- Push-ups (lagartijas)
- Sit-ups (abdominales)
- Run in place (correr, corre [s.], corran [pl.] en sitio)

- Jump in place (saltar, salta [s.], salten [pl.] en sitio)
- Bend (doblarse, doblate [s.], doblense [pl.])
- Turn (girar, gira [s.], giren [pl.])

Equipment Needed

Varies, depending on the skills that students will do; one die

Description

Create an oversized board game with different pathways (see example in figure 6.2). Each student will roll the die and move to the appropriate space. Each number on the board includes the number in Spanish and a fitness task also in Spanish that the student must complete.

Variations

Roll the die twice. The first number is for moving on the board and the second number is for the number of repetitions of the exercise to do.

Figure 6.2 A sample giant fitness board that you can use to play Fitness Board Game.

Omnikin Ball (Kin Ball) (Pelota Omnikin)

This cooperative game is played with an oversize ball and can be a great way to practice colors and other words in Spanish or sign language.

Words Learned

- Red (rojo)
- Green (verde)
- Blue (azul)
- White (blanco)
- Yellow (amarillo)
- One hand (una mano)
- Two hands (dos manos)

Equipment Needed

- A large Omnikin ball
- Pinnies (red, green, blue, yellow)

Description

There are four teams, each with a different color. Four players are on each team. The players of the defensive team form a square around the ball. The ball starts in the middle, and one team sets up to serve. The serving formation consists of two or three players kneeling down facing each other with heads down and arms outstretched. The ball is placed on their outstretched arms. The server approaches the Omnikin ball and says, "Omnikin," and then a color ("rojo") before striking the ball. When the color is announced and the ball is in the air, the corresponding team must catch the ball before it hits the ground. If the team whose color has been called does not catch the Omnikin ball before it hits the floor, then the striking team is awarded a point. The next team that serves the ball is the team whose color was just called whether they got the point or not. At the end, the team with the most points wins.

Variations

Use places as team names. Examples are the beach (playa), mountains (montañas), and ocean (mar).

Crossfire Cone Ball

The object of the game is to go into other teams' quadrants and knock over the bowling pin.

Words Learned

- Red (rojo)
- Green (verde)
- Blue (azul)
- White (blanco)

- Yellow (amarillo)
- Overhand (por arriba)
- Underhand (por abajo)

Equipment Needed

- 4 bowling pins
- Several gatorskin balls
- Pinnies for the 4 colors
- Cones (optional)
- Basket for basketball variation (optional)

Description

Divide the gym into four equal parts and place a bowling pin in each corner. The method for knocking over the bowling pin depends on your unit in physical education. Students can play the game using any of the rules for team handball, soccer, or football. You have the opportunity to work in the Spanish colors by calling out one to be attacked. When you blow the whistle and yell, "Rojo," the three other teams try to knock over the red pin while the red team plays defense. Students can also play this game using sign language: You or another student can sign the colors.

Variations

Replace the pins with two cones set up as a goal in each quadrant. So instead of trying to hit a pin, the players are required to pass a ball through the goal to a partner on the other side. This would open up the game for any attack game unit such as basketball, lacrosse, or field hockey. Another variation involves using Spanish names of foods, body parts, and so on for the team names.

Colors and Pathways (Colores y Caminos)

This game is ideal for the students to learn colors in Spanish and American sign language while playing an active game.

Words Learned

- Red (rojo)
- Green (verde)
- Blue (azul)
- Orange (naranja/anaranjado)

Equipment Needed

- Cones
- Frisbee
- Poly spots

Description

Form a circle with cones so that every person can have a spot next to a cone. A player throws a Frisbee to any person who is across from the thrower. Each cone has a different color assigned to it, and each color represents a locomotor skill. (For example, yellow means skip, and green means jump. Each locomotor skill can be written in Spanish on the colored paper on each cone.) The person who catches the Frisbee has to perform the locomotor skill designated for that color. Each color determines what locomotor skill to use over the poly spots that are arranged in a pattern within the circle. Once the person is finished performing the skill, he or she must choose another color of cone to stand next to. Movement is continuous throughout the activity so that students catch and immediately throw the Frisbee to another student. Once the students become more proficient in the activity, you can time the play to increase difficulty.

Variations

Use animals or time (tomorrow, yesterday, last week). Add more Frisbees for more movement.

seven
siete

High School Activities

The activities in this chapter focus on sport and recreation concepts. Students at this age must work on the foundation of sport and recreational skills. These dynamic sports, games, and activities incorporate word concepts, such as socialization, laterality, numbers, and places in a neighborhood, as well as relationships, such as family and friends. Every game in this book can be used with sign language or Spanish unless otherwise noted.

You should practice beforehand the words that you want to incorporate so you can instruct smoothly and clearly. Also, using visual and auditory input during instruction will ensure that children have a multisensory approach to learning sign language or Spanish or whatever language you choose to incorporate.

Action–Reaction (Acción–Reacción)

In the push-up position, students make decisions in a game situation on the commands given in sign language or Spanish.

Words Learned

- Red (rojo)
- Green (verde)
- Blue (azul)
- Any other color

Equipment Needed

Any objects that can be grabbed quickly (e.g., plastic floor-hockey pucks, tennis balls, large dice)

Description

Students with a partner are lined up facing one another. One object per group is placed on the floor directly in between the students partnered up. The students kneel down and wait for further instruction. Give the students the command "action" ("acción" in Spanish, or use the appropriate word in whatever other language you choose), after which the students assume the push-up position. Shortly after the "action" instruction, give the "reaction" command ("reacción" in Spanish), in which students try to grab the object before their partner does while holding themselves in the push-up position.

Variations

For younger students who might not be able to hold themselves up, they may just balance on all fours, or they can assume the sit-up position instead of the push-up position.

Another modification involves using three objects per set of partners. The objects can be of various colors, shapes, numbers, animal types, and so on that are clearly distinguishable from each other. Call out in Spanish or sign which object the students need to try to grab before their partner does. It is also a challenge to have the students grab the object with their eyes closed!

You can also play this game using sign language. Also, you can play this game in teams for points.

Very Nice to Meet You (Un Placer en Conocerte)

This is a get-to-know-you game. The students use sign language or Spanish as a medium for finding out facts about each other through various activities throughout the room.

Words Learned

- My name is (me llamo)
- I like to (me gusta)
- I am from (yo soy de)

Equipment Needed

None

Description

At the beginning of the activity, students are in a large circle. The object of this activity is to get to know the person to the left and the person to the right. When the activity begins, the students ask each other their names in sign language or in Spanish: "¿Cómo te llamas?" (What's your name?). Second, they ask each other to share something they like, using the phrase *me gusta* followed by a verb or noun: "Me gusta cantar" (I like to sing), "bailar" (to dance), "jugar" (to play), "estudiar" (to study), "el béisbol" (baseball), "la nieve" (the snow), "el verano" (the summer), "comer helado" (to eat ice cream). Finally, the students get to know each other a little more by asking each other, "De dónde eres tú?" (Where are you from?) They will answer, "Yo soy de" (I am from).

Variations

Instead of being in a circle, the students can be scattered around the gym. Then, you say a locomotor movement and the students get in pairs and interview their partners and switch to another locomotor movement to get to another partner.

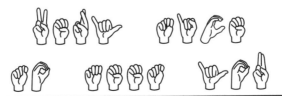

Red Light Green Light (Luz Roja Luz Verde) (Aquatic Activity)

In the deep end of the pool, one person has his back to the class while holding on to the wall or treading water. That person says, "Luz verde" ("green light" in Spanish) when he wants the group to swim toward him, and then "Luz roja" ("red light" in Spanish) when he wants the group to stop.

Words Learned

- Green (verde)
- Kick (patear, patea [s.], pateen [pl.])
- Fast (rápido)
- Yellow (amarillo)

- Slower (más despacio)
- Red (rojo)
- Stop (detenterse, detente [s.], deténganse [pl.])

Equipment Needed

Swimming pool

Description

Students hold on to the wall. Green light means the students should kick as hard and as fast as they can. Yellow light means they slow down their kick and create only small splashes. Red light means to stop.

Variations

Have fun switching up the cues quickly.

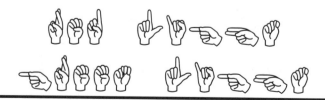

Bachata Dance (El Baile de la Bachata)

This traditional dance from the Dominican Republic can be used for practicing numbers and directions (laterality terms) in Spanish or sign language.

Words Learned

- One (uno)
- Two (dos)
- Three (tres)
- Tap (tocar, toca [s.], toquen [pl.])
- Right (derecha)
- Left (izquierda)

Equipment Needed

- CD player
- Bachata music

Description

Bachata is a dance that originated in the rural areas of the Dominican Republic. The music (also called bachata) is composed mostly of guitars and bass. For decades, bachata was banned from radio stations and television programs. Today bachata is one of the most popular music styles in the Dominican Republic as well as in other countries. Bachata is a very simple dance using four counts: uno, dos, tres, and tap (tocar, toca [s.], toquen [pl.]) on the fourth count. Instruct students on the dance: Move to the right beginning with the right foot, left, right, and tap with the left. Repeat the same to the left beginning with the left foot. You can also cue the students by using sign language. Cue the students either using numbers or the directions for the dance in Spanish or sign language. Once students learn the dance, they can provide the cues to the rest of the class.

Variations

Move to the right beginning with the right foot, left, right, and jump (saltar, salta [s.], salten [pl.]). Repeat the same to the left beginning with the left foot.

Moving the Hips Song (Moviendo las Caderas)

While listening to the song, students practice directions in Spanish or sign language after hearing or seeing the command.

Words Learned

- To the left (a la izquierda)
- To the right (a la derecha)
- Jump (saltar, salta [s.], salten [pl.])
- Slide (deslizarse, deslízate [s.], deslícense [pl.])
- Pause (detenerse, detente [s.], deténganse [pl.])

Equipment Needed

- CD player
- Music: The title of the song is "Moviendo las Caderas" by the Latin group Oro Solido. You can find this song on YouTube with the key words "Moviendo las Caderas song" or at this URL: www.youtube.com/watch?v=tiVFZS0GgaY.

Description

This is a dance activity that incorporates the hips and legs in swinging the hips left and right; it also involves jumping. The dance requires students to move to the left, then to the right ("a la izquierda, a la derecha") followed by a three-step count (uno, dos, tres). You can modify the steps by using various locomotor skills. When students become familiar with the steps and directions, they can get into groups of three or four and come up with a five-step count using left, right, and three other locomotor skills, such as jump (saltar, salta [s.], salten [pl.]), walk (caminar, camina [s.], caminen [pl.]), or gallop (galopar, galopa [s.], galopen [pl.]).

Variations

Students take turns leading this dance in Spanish or sign language. Also, you can use the Macarena dance or the cha-cha slide.

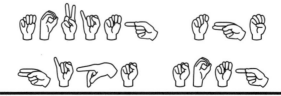

Four Squares (Cuatro Cuadros)

This game is similar to other invasion games (e.g., soccer or team handball), but the ball is thrown overhand or underhand. This game is a great way to learn and practice terms in Spanish or sign language related to colors, locomotor skills, and numbers.

Words Learned

- Underhand (por debajo)
- Overhand (por arriba)
- Red (rojo)
- Green (verde)
- Blue (azul)
- Yellow (amarillo)

Equipment Needed

- Pinnies
- Four-squares ball
- Cones or soccer goals

Description

Divide the students into four teams of three or four (use different-colored pinnies to make teams). The purpose of the activity is to score on any of the opponents' goals. The goals could be real soccer goals or cones. To move the ball, the students within the same team must pass the ball to each other without taking more than three steps. Give the teams various directions in Spanish (e.g., por arriba, por abajo) or sign language so that they can travel only in a certain direction while they attempt to score on the other teams' goals. Each team must also sign or say in Spanish the color of their team and the number of points they have. The team that has the most goals at the end of the game wins. You can modify the game so that the students pass the ball underhand (por debajo) or overhand (por arriba).

Variations

Practice volleyball skills, badminton skills, soccer skills (*patear* is to kick), or any other sport skills.

Volleyball Skills (Destrezas de Voleibol)

Students learn colors, animals, numbers, letters, and volleyball skill terminology in Spanish or sign language through this game (see figure 7.1).

Words Learned

- Numbers, letters, or animal labels in sign language
- Volleyball skills such as bump (bompear, bompea [s.], bompeen [pl.]), volley (volear, volea [s.], voleen [pl.]), serve (servir, sirve [s.], sirvan [pl.])

Equipment Needed

- Volleyballs
- Poly spots

Figure 7.1 Promoting Spanish and sign language in the Volleyball Skills game.

Description

Divide the class into groups of four or six. Give each team member a number, letter, or animal label. Each team stands at the wall behind a poly spot. You or a class member call out or sign a color, number, or animal of the team. Then you or the class member also say or sign the words for serve, bump, or volley (servir, bompear, volear). That team member will set up and do the volleyball skill against a wall.

Variations

Use basketball or any other sport skills such as soccer or badminton.

part III

Spanish and Sign Language Dictionaries

Part III presents basic terminology related to Spanish and sign language that you can use in your physical education classes.  The DVD included with this book contains the signs as well as pronunciation guidelines for some of the Spanish words used in this book. Also, all tables that appear in chapters 8 and 9 appear as reproducibles on the DVD.

Chapter 8 includes a variety of Spanish words to be used in physical education. Tips on pronouncing some of these words are also included. It is important to note that some of the words are presented in the infinitive form, whereas others are presented in the command form. For further information regarding verb conjugation, refer to the resources included at the end of this book. Also, you can identify a communication specialist in your school district, and in many cases the students themselves can be of great help in ensuring that the words are correctly pronounced. Chapter 9 presents a variety of American Sign Language signs organized by themes. If you need further assistance, check with interpreters, sign language teachers, and students themselves.

eight
ocho

Spanish Words
for Physical Education

All students, regardless of whether they are native speakers of the language in question, need to understand and be able to express themselves in a manner that is not only linguistically correct but socially appropriate. In order for people to understand another culture and speak the language, they need to understand ". . . conversational conventions such as greetings, farewells, form of address, thanking, making requests and giving or receiving compliments" (Peterson & Coltrane, 2003, p. 2).

You can help Hispanic students assimilate in your classes by using some Spanish words and by modeling appropriate social behavior within your own culture. This method helps English-speaking students understand the Hispanic students both linguistically and culturally. It creates a two-way learning process in which all students benefit by learning different ideologies, understanding a different culture, and gaining insight into their own culture.

Spanish and English differ greatly regarding number of phonemes. A phoneme is the smallest unit of sound that distinguishes a word in a particular language. While there is no absolute consensus among linguists, most agree that English has at least 13 pure vowel sounds (vowel phonemes), whereas Spanish has only 5 phonemes: A, E, I, O, U.

The five vowel phonemes in Spanish correspond to each vowel letter. The phonemes are represented by the symbols from the International Phonetic Alphabet (IPA), created by the International Phonetic Association, in which the letter remains as a letter and the phoneme is a symbol in brackets.

These are the five vowel letters and their corresponding phonemes in Spanish:

Letter	Phoneme
a	[a]
e	[e]
i	[i]
o	[o]
u	[u]

From L. Columna and L. Lieberman, 2011, *Promoting Language Through Physical Education* (Champaign, IL: Human Kinetics).

Spanish is a very phonetic language. That is, it is a language in which words are pronounced the way they are spelled and in which almost each letter corresponds to a specific sound with very few exceptions. Knowing the Spanish vowel phonemes will help anyone achieve appropriate pronunciation in a relatively short time.

To help you with your Spanish pronunciation, we have created a table that shows the vowel letters, their phonemes, and some words in English and Spanish in which those phonemes occur. The bold letters in the English words show where the Spanish phoneme occurs.

Letter	Phoneme	English words	Spanish words
a	[a]	comma; car; want; father	papa; casa; vaca; lata; cada; rata
e	[e]	met; pet; let; get; bread; spread Stressed vowels: hate; plate; fate	mesa; tela; métete; le; cera
i	[i]	bee; beach; bean; beef; these; geese	misa; tiza; risa; camisa; cita Teresita
o	[o]	predatory; coastal; stone; goat	cosa; moza toco; loco; manicomio; escritorio
u	[u]	boost; true; crew; booth; tooth; boo-hoo	uniforme; uso; puso; incluso; tubo

From L. Columna and L. Lieberman, 2011, *Promoting Language Through Physical Education* (Champaign, IL: Human Kinetics).

Each letter corresponds to one phoneme, and the phonemes do not change, regardless of what phoneme is before or after them. It is important to pronounce the vowels correctly in Spanish in order to communicate with your Hispanic students.

This chapter presents a list of physical education words with the Spanish translations in alphabetical order. The words can be organized in several ways; however, organizing the words in alphabetical order will assist you and your students in learning many words.

BODY PARTS

English	Spanish	English	Spanish	English	Spanish
abdomen	el abdomen	eyes	los ojos	knee	la rodilla
ankle	el tobillo	eyelids	los párpados	leg	la pierna
arm	el brazo	face	la cara	mouth	la boca
back	la espalda	finger	el dedo	muscle	el músculo
blood	la sangre	fingernails	las uñas	neck	el cuello
body	el cuerpo	foot/feet	el pie/los pies	nose	la nariz
bone	el hueso	forehead	la frente	shoulder	el hombro
cheek	la mejilla	gums	las encías	skin	la piel
chest	el pecho	hair	el cabello, el pelo	stomach	el estómago
chin	la barbilla	hand	la mano	throat	la garganta
ear	la oreja, el oído	head	la cabeza	toes	los dedos de los pies
elbow	el codo	heart	el corazón	tongue	la lengua
eyebrow	la ceja	heel	el talón	waist	la cintura
eyelashes	las pestañas	hip	la cadera	wrist	la muñeca

CLOTHING

English	Spanish	English	Spanish
raincoat	el impermeable	shorts	los pantalones cortos
ribbon	la cinta	skirt	la falda
scarf	la bufanda	socks	los calcetines, las medias
shirt	la camisa	tennis shoes	los zapatos de tenis
shoes	los zapatos	umbrella	el paraguas

GENDER AND POSSESSION

English	Spanish	English	Spanish
boys	niños	girls	niñas
my/mine	mi, mis (pl.)	your/yours	tu, tus (pl.)
his/her	su, sus (pl.)		

From L. Columna and L. Lieberman, 2011, *Promoting Language Through Physical Education* (Champaign, IL: Human Kinetics).

COLORS					
English	**Spanish**	**English**	**Spanish**	**English**	**Spanish**
DVD black	negro	*DVD* green	verde	*DVD* red	rojo
DVD blue	azul	*DVD* orange	naranja/anaranjado	white	blanco
DVD brown	castaño/marrón	*DVD* pink	rosado/rosa	*DVD* yellow	amarillo
gray	gris	*DVD* purple	morado/violeta		

DIRECTIONS					
English	**Spanish**	**English**	**Spanish**	**English**	**Spanish**
around	alrededor	open/closed	abierto/cerrado	Lie down here.	Acuéstate (s.)/ Acuéstense (pl.) aquí.
here/there	aquí/allá	*DVD* over	por encima	Please cover your mouth when you cough.	Cúbrete (s.)/ Cúbranse (pl.) la boca cuando tosas (s.)/tosan (pl.), por favor.
high/low	alto/bajo	this/that	este/ese	Please wait here.	Espera (s.)/ Esperen (pl.) aquí, por favor.
DVD in/out	adentro/afuera	*DVD* through	a través de	Please wash your hands.	Lávate (s.)/ Lávense (pl.) las manos, por favor.
large/small	grande/pequeño	*DVD* under	abajo de	Point to the spot where you have the pain.	Indícame (s.)/ Indíquenme (pl.) la parte donde te (s.)/ les (pl.) duele.
left/right	izquierdo/derecho (masculine), izquierda/derecha (feminine)	up/down	arriba/abajo	Sit here, please.	Siéntate (s.)/ Siéntense (pl.) aquí, por favor.
You are next.	Tú sigues.	Don't be afraid.	No tengas (s.)/ tengan (pl.) miedo.	Stand up.	Levántate (s.)/ Levántense (pl).

TELLING TIME					
English	**Spanish**	**English**	**Spanish**	**English**	**Spanish**
It's 1:00 (sharp).	Es la una (en punto).	It's 10:15.	Son las diez y cuarto. (. . . y quince).	It's 6:25.	Son las seis y veinticinco.
It's 7:00 (sharp).	Son las siete (en punto).	It's 4:45.	Son las cinco menos cuarto.	At what time . . . ?	¿A qué hora . . . ?
It's 3:30.	Son las tres y media.	It's 2:40.	Son las tres menos veinte.	What time is it?	¿Qué hora es?

From L. Columna and L. Lieberman, 2011, *Promoting Language Through Physical Education* (Champaign, IL: Human Kinetics).

EQUIPMENT

English	Spanish	English	Spanish	English	Spanish
DVD ball	la pelota, bola	goal	el arco, la portería	**DVD** soccer	el fútbol, balompié
bars	las barras	hopscotch	la peregrina, la rayuela, el tejo	sports	los deportes
DVD baseball	el béisbol	jump rope	el lazo de brincar, cuerda	sports field	el campo de deportes
basket	la canasta	marker	la marca	stadium	el estadio
DVD basketball	el baloncesto, basquetbol	net	la malla	sunglasses	las gafas del sol
DVD bat	el bate	picnic	el día de campo	swimming pool	la piscina, la alberca
bench	el banco	player	el jugador	swings	los columpios
camera	la camara	playground	el patio de recreo, el patio	team	el equipo
cone	el cono	playground rules	las reglas del patio de recreo	teeter-totter	el sube y baja
equipment	el equipo	racket	la raqueta	tennis court	la cancha de tenis
fence	el cercado de alambre, la cerca	recess	el recreo	track and field	pista y campo
field trip	el paseo, la excursión	ribbon	la medalla	umpire	el árbitro
DVD football	el fútbol americano	rings	los anillos	wagon	el vagón, el carrito
game	el juego	sandbox	la caja de arena, el arenero	wand	la varita
game, sports	el partido	slide	el resbaladero, chorrera, resbaladilla		

FAMILY

English	Spanish	English	Spanish	English	Spanish
aunt	tía	grandfather	abuelo	parents	padres
brother	hermano	grandmother	abuela	sister	hermana
child	niño(a)	grandson	nieto	son	hijo
cousin	primo(a)	husband	esposo	uncle	tío
daughter	hija	mother	mamá	wife	esposa
father	papá	nephew	sobrino		
granddaughter	nieta	niece	sobrina		

To change a word from singular to plural in Spanish, if the singular word ends in a vowel, you simply have to add an *s* (e.g., sobrina to sobrinas). If the singular word ends in a consonant, then you simply have to add *es*. In this particular table, the words all end in a vowel, so you only need to add the *s*. The only exception is the word padres, which is already in the plural form.

From L. Columna and L. Lieberman, 2011, *Promoting Language Through Physical Education* (Champaign, IL: Human Kinetics).

DAYS OF THE WEEK

English	Spanish	English	Spanish	English	Spanish
Monday	el lunes	Thursday	el jueves	Saturday	el sábado
Tuesday	el martes	Friday	el viernes	Sunday	el domingo
Wednesday	el miércoles				

MONTHS OF THE YEAR

English	Spanish	English	Spanish	English	Spanish
January	enero	May	mayo	September	septiembre
February	febrero	June	junio	October	octubre
March	marzo	July	julio	November	noviembre
April	abril	August	agosto	December	diciembre

GREETINGS

English	Spanish	English	Spanish	English	Spanish
Are you the mother (father)?	¿Es usted la mamá (el papá)?	How are you? (formal)	¿Cómo está usted (s.)/están ustedes (pl.)?	So-so.	Más o menos; Así-así.
Are you the parents of the child?	¿Son ustedes los padres del niño?	How are you? (informal)	Cómo estás (s.)/ están (pl.)?	Thank you for your help.	Gracias por su ayuda.
Do you speak English? (formal)	¿Habla usted inglés?	How many?	¿Cuánto(a)s?	Until I see you again.	Hasta la vista.
Excuse me.	Discúlpeme (formal)/ Discúlpame (informal)/ Discúlpenme (pl.).	How old are you?	¿Cuántos años tienes?	Until tomorrow.	Hasta mañana.
Fine, thanks. And you? (formal)	Bien, gracias. ¿Y usted (s.)/ ustedes (pl.)?	How old is he (she)?	¿Cuántos años tiene?	Very well.	Muy bien.
Fine, thanks. And you? (informal)	Bien, gracias. ¿Y tú?	How?	¿Cómo?	What is your child's name?	¿Cómo se llama el(la) niño(a)?
From where?	¿De dónde?	I am ____ years old.	Tengo ____ años.	What is your name?	¿Cómo te llamas?
Good afternoon.	Buenas tardes.	I'm fine, thank you.	Estoy bien, gracias.	What?	¿Qué?
Good-bye.	Adiós.	My name is ____.	Me llamo ____.		
Good evening.	Buenas noches.	**DVD** Please.	Por favor.		
Good morning. My name is ____.	Buenos días. Me llamo ____.	Pretty well.	Bastante bien.		
Hello.	Hola (*h* is silent).	See you later.	Hasta luego.		

From L. Columna and L. Lieberman, 2011, *Promoting Language Through Physical Education* (Champaign, IL: Human Kinetics).

NUMBERS					
English	Spanish	English	Spanish	English	Spanish
0	cero	20	veinte	101	ciento uno
1	uno	21	veintiuno	200	doscientos
2	dos	22	veintidós	300	trescientos
3	tres	23	veintitrés	400	cuatrocientos
4	cuatro	24	veinticuatro	500	quinientos
5	cinco	25	veinticinco	600	seiscientos
6	seis	26	veintiséis	700	setecientos
7	siete	27	veintisiete	800	ochocientos
8	ocho	28	veintiocho	900	novecientos
9	nueve	29	veintinueve	1000	mil
10	diez	30	treinta	1st	primero(a)
11	once	31	treinta y uno	2nd	segundo(a)
12	doce	32	treinta y dos	3rd	tercero(a)
13	trece	40	cuarenta	4th	cuarto(a)
14	catorce	50	cincuenta	5th	quinto(a)
15	quince	60	sesenta	6th	sexto(a)
16	dieciséis	70	setenta	7th	séptimo(a)
17	diecisiete	80	ochenta	8th	octavo(a)
18	dieciocho	90	noventa	9th	noveno(a)
19	diecinueve	100	cien	10th	décimo(a)

From L. Columna and L. Lieberman, 2011, *Promoting Language Through Physical Education* (Champaign, IL: Human Kinetics).

English	Spanish	English	Spanish	English	Spanish
_____ is paying attention.	_____ está (s.)/están (pl.) prestando atención.	I like the way _____ is sitting quietly.	Me gusta la manera en que _____ está (s.)/están (pl.) sentado en silencio.	That's coming along nicely.	Eso está resultando muy bien.
_____ has the answer.	_____ tiene la respuesta.	I like the way you are working.	Me gusta la manera en que estás (s.)/están (pl.) trabajando.	That's good.	Eso está bien.
Congratulations.	Felicidades.	I'm proud of the way you are working today.	Estoy muy orgulloso(a) de la manera en que estás (s.)/están (pl.) trabajando hoy.	That's great!	¡Eso es maravilloso! ¡Tremendo!
Continue your good work.	Sigue (continúa) con el buen trabajo.	I'm sure your mom and dad would be proud to see the job you did on this.	Estoy seguro(a) que tu papá y mamá estarían orgullosos de ver este trabajo que hiciste (s.)/hicieron (pl.).	That's interesting.	Eso es interesante.
Everyone's working so hard.	Todos están trabajando con mucho empeño.	It's a pleasure to teach when you work like this.	Es un placer enseñar cuando trabajas (s.)/trabajan (pl.) así.	That's quite an improvement.	Eso es un gran adelanto.
Exactly right!	Perfectamente correcto.	Keep up the good work.	Sigue (pl. sigan) adelante con tu buen trabajo.	That's really nice.	Eso está realmente bien.
Excellent work.	Excelente trabajo.	Marvelous.	Maravilloso.	That's right!	Está correcto!
Fantastic!	¡Fantástico!	Much better.	Mucho mejor.	Very creative.	Muy creativo.
Fine.	Bien.	Now you've figured it out.	Ya lo figuraste.	Very good.	Muy bien.
Good idea.	Buena idea.	Superior work. Why don't you show the class?	Trabajo superior. ¿Por qué no le muestras a la clase?	Very interesting.	Muy interesante.
DVD Good job.	Buen trabajo.	Terrific!	¡Estupendo!	What neat work.	¡Qué trabajo tan limpio!
How impressive!	¡Qué impresionante!	**DVD** Thank you.	Gracias.	You are a good student.	Tú eres un(a) buen(a) estudiante.
How nice!	¡Qué bien!	Thank you for raising your hand.	Gracias por levantar la mano.	You did well.	Hiciste muy bien.
I appreciate your help.	Aprecio tu ayuda.	That is the correct answer.	Esa es la respuesta correcta.	You made only one mistake.	Solamente hiciste un error.
I congratulate you.	Te felicito.	That's a good point.	Eso es un buen punto.	You make it look easy.	Tú (s.)/Ustedes (pl.) lo haces (s.)/hacen (pl.) parecer fácil.

From L. Columna and L. Lieberman, 2011, *Promoting Language Through Physical Education* (Champaign, IL: Human Kinetics).

QUESTIONS

English	Spanish	English	Spanish	English	Spanish
What is your name?	¿Cómo te llamas?	Don't you feel well?	¿No te sientes bien?	Have you had this kind of sickness before?	¿Has tenido este tipo de enfermedad antes?
What happened?	¿Qué pasó?	Why don't you feel well?	¿Por qué no te sientes bien?	Are you taking any medicine?	¿Estás tomando alguna medicina?
How did you get hurt?	¿Cómo te lastimaste?	How long have you been sick?	¿Cuánto tiempo hace que estás enfermo(a)?	Do you want to go to the bathroom?	¿Quieres ir al baño?
Where do you hurt?	¿Qué te duele?	Were you sick last night?	¿Estabas enfermo(a) anoche?	Are you nauseated?	¿Estás con náuseas?
What's the matter?	¿Qué te pasa? ¿Qué tienes?	Do you feel bad?	¿Te sientes mal?	Did you eat breakfast today?	¿Desayunaste hoy?
Are you sick?	¿Estás enfermo(a)?	Do you have a stomach ache?	¿Tienes dolor de estómago?	Have you taken any kind of drugs?	¿Has tomado cualquier tipo de medicinas?
How do you feel?	¿Cómo te sientes?	Do you have a cold?	¿Tienes catarro/ resfriado?		

SEASONS AND WEATHER

English	Spanish	English	Spanish	English	Spanish
summer	el verano	It's hot.	Hace calor.	thunder	el trueno
fall	el otoño	It's raining.	Está lloviendo.	weather	el tiempo
winter	el invierno	It's sunny.	Hace sol.	wind	el viento
spring	la primavera	It's windy.	Hace viento.	The weather is bad.	Hace mal tiempo.
It's cloudy.	Está nublado.	sun	el sol	The weather is good.	Hace buen tiempo.
It's cold.	Hace frío.	temperature	la temperatura	What's the weather like?	¿Qué tiempo hace?

From L. Columna and L. Lieberman, 2011, *Promoting Language Through Physical Education* (Champaign, IL: Human Kinetics).

VERBS					
English	**Spanish**	**English**	**Spanish**	**English**	**Spanish**
answer	contestar (contesta [s.], contesten [pl.])	dance	bailar (baila [s.], bailen [pl.])	hang up	colgar (cuelga [s.], cuelguen [pl.])
arrive	llegar (llega [s.], llegen [pl.])	define	definir (define [s.], definan [pl.])	**DVD** help	ayudar (ayuda [s.], ayuden [pl.])
ask	preguntar (pregunta [s.], pregunten [pl.])	describe	describir (describe [s.], describan [pl.])	hold	agarrar, sujetar (agarra/sujeta [s.], agarren/sujeten [pl.])
begin	comenzar, empezar (comienza/empieza [s.], comiencen/empiecen [pl.])	dodge	esquivar (esquiva [s.], esquiven [pl.])	hunt for	buscar (busca [s.], busquen [pl.])
call	llamar (llama [s.], llamen [pl.])	draw	dibujar (dibuja [s.], dibujen [pl.])	**DVD** kick	patear (patea [s.], pateen [pl.])
can, to be able	poder (puedes [s.], pueden [pl.])	dribble	driblear, botar (driblea/bota [s.], dribleen/boten [pl.])	learn	aprender (aprende [s.], aprendan [pl.])
carry, take	llevar (lleva [s.], lleven [pl.])	drink	beber, tomar (bebe/toma [s.], beban/tomen [pl.])	leave	salir (sal [s.], salgan [pl.])
DVD catch	atrapar (atrapa [s.], atrapen [pl.])	eat	comer (come [s.], coman [pl.])	leave from	irse (véte [s.], váyanse [pl.])
chase	perseguir (persigue [s.], persigan [pl.])	erase	borrar (borra [s.], borren [pl.])	lie down	acostarse (acuéstate [s.], acuéstense [pl.])
clean	limpiar (limpia [s.], limpien [pl.])	fill	llenar (llena [s.], llenen [pl.])	**DVD** like	gustar (me gusta jugar) (te gusta jugar [s.], les gusta jugar [pl.])
climb	subir (sube [s.], suban [pl.])	find	encontrar (encuentra [s.], encuentren [pl.])	listen	escuchar (escucha [s.], escuchen [pl.])
close	cerrar (cierra [s.], cierren [pl.])	finish	terminar (termina [s.], terminen [pl.])	look at	mirar (mira [s.], miren [pl.])
color	colorear (colorea [s.], coloreen [pl.])	flee	huir (huye [s.], huyan [pl.])	make	hacer (haz [s.], hagan [pl.])
complete	acabar, completar (acaba/completa [s.], acaben/completen [pl.])	fly	volar (vuela [s.], vuelen [pl.])	measure	medir (mide [s.], midan [pl.])
correct	corregir (corrige [s.], corrijan [pl.])	form	formar (forma [s.], formen [pl.])	mix	mezclar (mezcla [s.], mezclen [pl.])
count	contar (cuenta [s.], cuenten [pl.])	**DVD** gallop	galopar (galopa [s.], galopen [pl.])	move	mover (mueve [s.], muevan [pl.])
cover	cubrir, tapar (cubre/tapa [s.], cubran/tapen [pl.])	get up	levantarse (leván-tate [s.], levántense [pl.])	open	abrir (abre [s.], abran [pl.])
cross out	tachar (tacha [s.], tachen [pl.])	give	dar (da [s.], den [pl.])	paint	pintar (pinta [s.], pinten [pl.])
cut	cortar (corta [s.], corten [pl.])	go	ir (ve [s.], vayan [pl.])	**DVD** pass	pasar (pasa [s.], pasen [pl.])

A verb in the infinitive (verbs that have not been conjugated into any particular person) is a verb in its purest form and it is the equivalent to to go, to do, to play in English, and so on. When you conjugate a verb, you are putting it in a form that is for a specific person in a given tense. Most of the time, while in a physical education class, you will use the command form of the verb and you will need to use this form in singular and in plural.

From L. Columna and L. Lieberman, 2011, *Promoting Language Through Physical Education* (Champaign, IL: Human Kinetics).

English	Spanish	English	Spanish	English	Spanish
pay	pagar (paga [s.], paguen [pl.])	return (an object)	devolver (devuelve [s.], devuelvan [pl.])	sleep	dormirse (duérmete [s.], duérmanse [pl.])
DVD pay attention	prestar atención, poner atención (presta/pon atención [s.], presten/pongan atención [pl.])	roll	dar vueltas (da vueltas [s.], den vueltas [pl.])	slide	deslizarse (deslízate [s.], deslícense [pl.])
pick up	recoger (recoge [s.], rocojan [pl.])	**DVD** run	correr (corre [s.], corran [pl.])	speak	hablar (habla [s.], hablen [pl.])
pin	prender (prende [s.], prendan [pl.])	save	guardar (guarda [s.], guarden [pl.])	spell	deletrear (deletrea [s.], deletreen [pl.])
play	jugar (juega [s.], jueguen [pl.])	say	decir (di [s.], digan [pl.])	**DVD** stand up	pararse, ponerse en pie (párate/ponte de pie [s.], párense/pónganse de pie [pl.])
punctuate	poner los puntos (pon los puntos [s.], pongan los puntos [pl.])	see	ver (ve [s.], vean [pl.])	start	comenzar, empezar (comienza/empieza [s.], comiencen/empiecen [pl.])
put away	guardar (guarda [s.], guarden [pl.])	send	mandar, enviar (manda/envía [s.], manden/envíen [pl.])	**DVD** stop	parar (para [s.], paren [pl.])
rain	llover (llueve [s.])	set	poner, colocar (pon/coloca [s.], pongan/coloquen [pl.])	stretch	estirarse (estírate [s.], estírense [pl.])
read	leer (lee [s.], lean [pl.])	show	mostrar (muestra [s.], muestren [pl.])	strike with a racket	pegar, golpear con una raqueta (pégale/golpéale con la raqueta [s.], péguenle/golpéenle con la raqueta [pl.])
remember	recordar (recuerda [s.], recuerden [pl.])	shut	cerrar (cierra [s.], cierren [pl.])	study	estudiar (estudia [s.], estudien [pl.])
rest	descansar (descansa [s.], descansen [pl.])	sing	cantar (canta [s.], canten [pl.])	**DVD** swim	nadar (nada [s.], naden [pl.])
return (to a place)	volver (vuelve [s.], vuelvan [pl.])	**DVD** sit down	sentarse (siéntate [s.], siéntense [pl.])	swing	balancearse (balancéate [s.], balancéense [pl.])

From L. Columna and L. Lieberman, 2011, *Promoting Language Through Physical Education* (Champaign, IL: Human Kinetics).

(continued)

VERBS CONTINUED					
English	Spanish	English	Spanish	English	Spanish
take notes	tomar notas, tomar apuntes (toma notas/ apuntes [s.], tomen notas/ apuntes [pl.])	trace	delinear delinea [s.], delineen [pl.])	wait	esperar (espera [s.], esperen [pl.])
teach	enseñar (enseña [s.], enseñen [pl.])	travel	viajar (viaja [s.], viajen [pl.])	**DV** walk, go for a walk	andar, caminar (anda/camina [s.], anden/ caminen [pl.])
tear	romper (rompe [s.], rompan [pl.])	try	tratar (trata [s.], traten [pl.])	wash (oneself)	lavar(se) (lávate [s.], lávense [pl.])
tell (say)	decir (di [s.], digan [pl.])	turn around	dar vuelta (da vuelta[s] [s.], den vuelta[s] [pl.])	watch out	tener cuidado (ten cuidado [s.], tengan cuidado [pl.])
tell (relate)	contar (cuenta [s.], cuenten [pl.])	twist	girar (gira [s.], giren [pl.])	win	ganar (gana [s.], ganen [pl.])
think	pensar (piensa [s.], piensen [pl.])	underline	subrayar (subraya [s.], subrayen [pl.])	work	trabajar (trabaja [s.], trabajen [pl.])
DV throw	tirar, lanzar (tira/ lanza [s.], tiren/ lancen [pl.])	use	usar (usa [s.], usen [pl.])	write	escribir (escribe [s.], escriban [pl.])
tie	amarrar (amarra [s.], amarren [pl.])	visit	visitar (visita [s.], visiten [pl.])		
touch	tocar (toca [s.], toquen [pl.])	volley	volear (volea [s.], voleen [pl.])		

From L. Columna and L. Lieberman, 2011, *Promoting Language Through Physical Education* (Champaign, IL: Human Kinetics).

nine
nueve

ASL Signs
for Physical Education

This chapter contains a list of physical education words and their corresponding signs organized by theme (e.g., sports, execution feedback, directions, colors, games terminology, formations).

Sign Language Related to Physical Education

Words and Phrases

DVD Help

DVD Thank you.

DVD I'm sorry.

Execution Feedback

Good

Better

Directions

Come

DVD In

More Physical Education Vocabulary

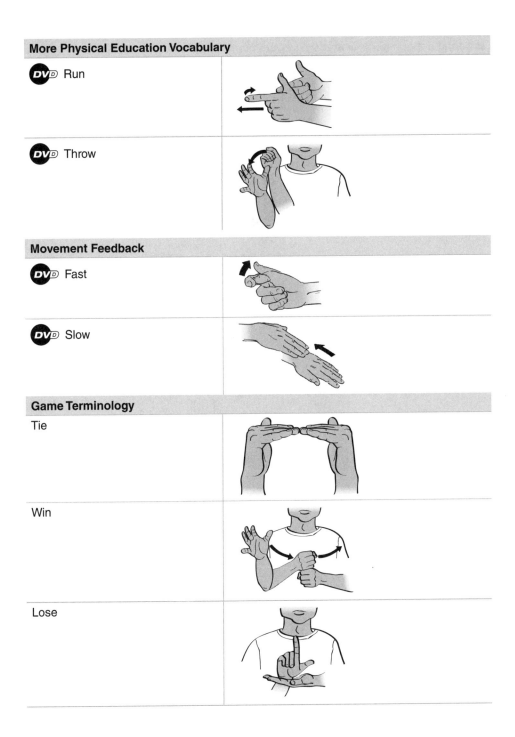

DVD Run

DVD Throw

Movement Feedback

DVD Fast

DVD Slow

Game Terminology

Tie

Win

Lose

Physical Education Formations and Commands

DVD Stop	
Finish	
DVD Look at me	
DVD Line up	

Feelings

DVD Happy	
DVD Sad	
DVD Angry	

Items and Gender

Boy	
Girl	
Bicycle	

Colors

DVD Blue	
DVD Red	
DVD Black	

appendix A

Resources

Following is a list of websites that you can use as a supplement to the information presented in this book. A description of each website is provided.

SIGN LANGUAGE WEBSITES	
Web address	**Description**
http://commtechlab.msu.edu/sites/aslweb/browser.html	ASL Browser provides videos for each word in sign language. Written descriptions are also included. PE terminology (e.g., run, jump) can also be found on this site.
www.handspeak.com	This sign language site includes several features (e.g., word of the day and a phrase of the week). It also explains grammar of ASL.
www.masterstech-home.com/aSLDict.html	This is a basic dictionary of ASL terms. The site provides videos for each word in sign language as well as written descriptions of how to perform the signs.
www.aslpro.com	This site is a free resource for teachers. You can create accounts and personalize a quiz for students' use, then let them practice.

SPANISH LANGUAGE WEBSITES	
Web address	**Description**
www.uni.edu/becker/Spanish3.html	This site is for educators and students. It includes sections in which you can practice Spanish grammar and receive help with Spanish verbs.
www.languagelearninglibrary.org/spanish	This site includes grammar tips, common phrases, numbers, and links in various languages.
www.ielanguages.com/spanish.html	This site includes pronunciation and grammar rules for Spanish.
www.ctspanish.com/sports/sports.htm	This is an excellent site with vocabulary in Spanish and English about the most common sports.
www.123teachme.com/learn_spanish/teachers_parents_students	123 TeachMe contains Spanish phrases for teachers to use with parents and students. Pronunciations are also included.
http://translate.google.com/#	This site allows you to type in a word in English or Spanish (or any other language) and have it translated to your choice of any other language.

From L. Columna and L. Lieberman, 2011, *Promoting Language Through Physical Education* (Champaign, IL: Human Kinetics).

appendix B

Softball Homework Sheet
Asignación de Softball

Instructions: Practice the following words in Spanish and English for next class. We'll practice this vocabulary every day before class.

Instrucciones: Practica las siguientes palabras en español y en inglés para la próxima clase. Practicaremos este vocabulario todos los días antes de comenzar la clase.

English word (palabra en inglés)	Spanish word (palabra en español)
first base	primera base
second base	segunda base
third base	tercera base
home plate	plato
helmet	casco
bat	bate
ball	pelota

From L. Columna and L. Lieberman, 2011, *Promoting Language Through Physical Education* (Champaign, IL: Human Kinetics).

(continued)

(continued)

English word (palabra en inglés)	Spanish word (palabra en español)
batter	bateador
catcher	receptor
pitcher	lanzador
glove	guante
strike zone strike zone	zona de strike

From L. Columna and L. Lieberman, 2011, *Promoting Language Through Physical Education* (Champaign, IL: Human Kinetics).

references

Aud, S., Hussar, W., Planty, M., Snyder, T., Bianco, K., Fox, M., Frohlich, L., Kemp, J., & Drake, L. (2010). The condition of education 2010 (NCES 2010-028). National Center for Education Statistics, Institute of Education Sciences, U.S. Department of Education. Washington, DC. http://nces.ed.gov/programs/coe/2010/pdf/6_2010.pdf.

Bain, L., Scott, S., & Steinberg, A.G. (2004). Socialization experiences and coping strategies of adults raised using spoken language. *Journal of Deaf Studies and Deaf Education, 9*(1), 120-128.

Bruner, J. (1983). *Child's talk: Learning to use language.* New York: Norton.

Burton, L.J., & VanHeest, J.L. (2007). The importance of physical activity in closing the achievement gap. *Quest, 59*(2), 212-218.

Cagle, C.S. (2006). Student understanding of culturally and ethically responsive care: Implications for nursing curricula. *Nursing Education Perspectives, 27*(6), 308-314.

Cenoz, J., & Genesee, F. (1998). *Beyond bilingualism: Multilingualism and multilingual education.* Bristol, UK: Multilingual Matters.

Culp, B.O., Chepyator-Thomson, J.R., & Hsu, S.H. (2009). Pre-service teachers' experiential perspectives based on a multicultural learning service practicum. *Physical Educator, 66*(1), 23-36.

Davis Lensky, S., Ehlers-Zavala, F., Daniel, M.C., & Sun-Irminger, X. (2006). Assessing English-language learners in mainstream classrooms. *International Reading Association, 60*, 24-34.

Deaflympics, Inc. (2005, January). Constitution. www.deaflympics.com/about/index.asp?DID=545.

Ellis, M.K. (2001). Influence of parental hearing levels and school placement on the health-related physical fitness and community sports involvement of children who are deaf. *Palaestra, 17*(1), 44-49.

Estrada, V., Gómez, L., & Ruiz-Escalante, J.A. (2009). Let's make dual language the norm. *Educational Leadership, 66*(7), 54-58.

Foster, S. (1998). Communication as social engagement: Implications for interactions between deaf and hearing persons. *Scandinavian Audiology, 27*(49), 116-124.

Gay, G. (2000). *Culturally responsive teaching: Theory, research, and practice.* New York: Teachers College Press.

Gay, G., & Howard, T.C. (2000). Multicultural teacher education for the 21st century. *Teacher Educator, 36*(1), 1-16.

Goodman, J., & Hopper, C. (1992). Hearing impaired children and youth: A review of psychomotor behavior. *Adapted Physical Activity Quarterly, 9*, 214-236.

Hearing Loss Association (HLA). (2007). Facing the challenge. www.hearinglossca.org/html/booklet.htm#stat.

Lee, S.J., & Kumashiro, K.K. (2005). *A report on the status of Asian Americans and Pacific Islanders in education: Beyond the "model minority" stereotype.* Washington, DC: National Education Association.

Lieberman, L.J., Columna, L., Martínez de la Vega Mansilla, P., & Taylor, C. (2010). Infusing sign language and Spanish into physical education. *Journal of Physical Education Recreation and Dance 81*(4), 45-49.

Marschark, M. (1997). *Psychological development of deaf children.* New York: Oxford University Press.

McCollum, S., Civalier, A., & Holt, A. (2004). Equitable learning for Spanish speaking students in elementary physical education. *Strategies, 17*(6), 21-23.

McGehee, R.V. (2004). Latino sport. In Duncan, J.D. (Ed.), *From Ali to X-Games in American Culture* (211- 212). Santa Barbara: ABC-CLIO.

Mertens, D. (1989). Social experiences of hearing-impaired high school youth. *American Annals of the Deaf, 134*(1), 15-19.

Moores, D. (2001). *Educating the deaf.* 5th ed. Boston: Houghton Mifflin.

National Association for the Education of Young Children (NAEYC). (1995). *Responding to linguistic and cultural diversity recommendations for effective early childhood education.* Washington, DC: Author.

National Commission on Teaching and America's Future. (1996). *What matters most: Teaching for America's future.* New York: Author.

Obama, B. (2010, September 15). National Hispanic Heritage Month. A proclamation. www.whitehouse.gov/the-press-office/2010/09/15/presidential-proclamation-national-hispanic-heritage-month.

O'Malley, J.M., & Valdez Pierce, L. (1996). *Authentic assessment for English language learners: Practical approaches for teachers.* Reading, MA: Addison Wesley.

Owers, R. (1996). Hearing children's attitudes towards deafness. *Journal of the British Association of Teachers of the Deaf, 20*(3), 83-89.

Parasnis, I. (2000). *Deaf ethnic-minority students: Diversity and identity.* CD-ROM Proceedings of the 19th International Congress on Education of the Deaf and 7th Asia-Pacific Congress on Deafness. Sydney, Australia.

Pender, R.H., & Patterson, P.E. (1982). A comparison of selected motor fitness items between congenitally deaf and hearing children. *Journal of Special Educators, 18*(4), 71-75.

Peterson, E., & Coltrane, B. (2003). Culture in second language teaching. *Eric Digest* EDO-FL-03-09. Center for Applied Linguistics. www.cal.org/resources/digest/digest_pdfs/0309peterson.pdf.

Schirmer, B.R. (2001). *Psychological, social, and educational dimensions of deafness.* Boston: Allyn and Bacon.

Stewart, D.A. (1991). *Deaf sport: The impact of sports within the deaf community.* Washington, DC: Gallaudet University Press.

Stewart, D.A., Dummer, G.M., & Haubenstricker, J.L. (1990). Review of administration procedures used to assess the motor skills of deaf children and youth. *Adapted Physical Activity Quarterly, 7*(3), 231-239.

Stewart, D.A., & Ellis, M.K. (1999). Physical education for deaf students. *American Annals of the Deaf, 144*(4), 315-319.

Stewart, D.A., & Ellis, M.K. (2006). Revisiting the role of physical education for deaf children. In *Deaf learners: New developments in curriculum and instruction.* (D.F. Moores & D.S. Martin, Eds.). Washington, DC: Gallaudent University Press.

Stewart, D.A., Robinson, J.H., & McCarthy, D. (1991). Participation in Deaf sport: Characteristics of elite athletes. *Adapted Physical Activity Quarterly, 8,* 136-145.

Stinson, M.S., & Whitmire, K. (1996). Self-perceptions of social relationships in hearing-impaired adolescents. *Journal of Educational Psychology, 88*(1), 132-143.

Tvingstedt, A.L. (1995, July). *Classroom interaction and the social situation of hard-of-hearing pupils in regular classes.* Paper presented at the 18th International Congress on Education of the Deaf, Tel Aviv, Israel.

U.S. Census Bureau. (2009). Hispanic population of the United States. www.census.gov/population/www/socdemo/hispanic/hispanic_pop_presentation.html.

U.S. Department of Education. In RE: President's Commission on Excellence in Special Education Accountability Systems Task Force. Proceedings, Des Moines, IA, March 13, 2002.

Vakil, S., Freeman, R., & Swim, T.J. (2003). The Reggio Emila approach and inclusive early childhood programs. *Early Childhood Education Journal, 30,* 187-192.

Vialle, W., & Paterson, J. (1998). Deafening silence: The educational experiences of gifted deaf people. *Gifted Education International, 13*(1), 13-22.

Wilford, S. (2003). Sharing the power of play with parents. *Scholastic Early Childhood Today, 18*(2), 10-11.

Winnick, J.P., & Short, F.X. (1985). Physical fitness testing of the disabled. *Project Unique.* Champaign, IL: Human Kinetics.

about the authors

Luis Columna, PhD, is an associate professor at Syracuse University in Syracuse, New York. Armed with three degrees in adapted physical education and physical education, Columna is intent on helping teachers work better with diverse learners. He has taught in private and public schools in Texas and Puerto Rico and has taught higher education since 2006. Along with his coauthor, he has conducted several workshops and written several articles related to promoting language.

Columna, who infuses Spanish in his courses, is the chair-elect of the National Adapted Physical Activity Council (APAC). He was the editor of the APAC section in the journal *Palaestra*. He is also a member of the Social Justice and Cultural Diversity Committee of the National Association of Kinesiology and Physical Education in Higher Education. In 2011, Columna was the recipient of the Social Justice and Diversity Young Professional Award from the American Alliance for Health, Physical Education, Recreation and Dance. In his spare time, Columna enjoys dancing, traveling, and hiking.

Lauren J. Lieberman, PhD, is a professor at The College at Brockport in Brockport, New York. She has taught higher education since 1995 and taught in Perkins School for the Blind since 2010. She is fluent in sign language, using sign as her language in earning her PhD. She infuses sign language throughout her courses.

Lieberman has written 11 books on adapted physical education and started Camp Abilities, a developmental sports camp for children with visual impairments. This camp is now replicated in eight states and two countries.

Lieberman is past chair of the National Adapted Physical Activity Council (APAC), and she serves on the board of the U.S. Association for Blind Athletes. She acts as a consultant for the New York State Deafblind Collaborative. In her leisure time, she enjoys playing ultimate, biking, running, kayaking, hiking, and playing the guitar.

DVD-ROM User Instructions

System Requirements

Microsoft Windows

- Windows 2000/XP/Vista/Windows7
- Adobe Reader 8 or above
- Printer

Macintosh

- MAC OSX (any version)
- Printer

User Instructions

The PDFs on this DVD-ROM can only be accessed using a DVD-ROM drive in a computer (not a DVD player on a television). To access the PDF, follow these instructions:

Microsoft Windows

1. Place DVD in the DVD-ROM drive of your computer.
2. Double-click on the **My Computer** icon on your desktop.
3. Right-click on the DVD-ROM drive and select the **Open** option from the pop-up menu.
4. Double-click on the **Documents and Resources** folder.
5. Select the PDF file that you want to view or print.

Macintosh

1. Place DVD in the DVD-ROM drive of your computer.
2. Double-click on the DVD icon on your desktop.
3. Double-click on the **Documents and Resources** folder.
4. Select the PDF file that you want to view or print.

Note: You must have Adobe Acrobat Reader to view the PDF files.

For customer support, contact Technical Support:

Phone: 217-351-5076, Option 3, Monday through Friday (excluding holidays) between 7:00 a.m. to 7:00 p.m. (CST).

E-mail: support@hkusa.com